Fifty Plus Memories:
Conversations About the Past

Collected contributions from members and friends of the Montague 50 Plus Club of Prince Edward Island, Canada

Copyright 2017 by The Montague 50+ Club. No part of this book may be used in any form or by any means graphical, electronic, or mechanical without written permission of the copyright owner.

Each contributor participated willingly and has implicitly provided the 50+ club with a license to use their conversations, writing, or photographs in this or subsequent printings of this book. For purposes of copyright, each person retains the rights to their individual contributions.

ISBN: 978-1-987852-09-7

First printing January 2017

Publisher: Wood Island Prints; 670 Trans-Canada Highway, RR1; Belle River, PE C0A 1B0; (902) 962-3335; schultz@pei.sympatico.ca; www.woodislandsprints.com

Printing: Lightning Source Inc. (US); 1246 Heil Quaker Blvd, La Vergne, TN 37086; USA; (615) 213-5815
inquiry@lightningsource.com; www.lightningsource.com

Additional copies of this book may be obtained from the Montague 50+ Club or may be ordered through www.amazon.com

This book was developed with the aid of a grant from the PEI Senior's Secretariat.

INTRODUCTION:
HOW THIS BOOK CAME TO BE

The 50+ Club in Montague, PEI, Canada was desperately searching for someone to accept the position of president for the 2014 year, and, I later learned, they had gone through 10 names before they got to me. Naively thinking I could streamline their monthly meetings and make a other changes, I accepted the nomination, which was tantamount to election in these (not) hotly contested races. I spent a few months trying to figure things out. A book title, *The Seven Last Words of the Church: We've Never Done It That Way Before*, fit the way things went. I was both a newcomer to the club and someone 'from away'. There is inherent inertia in any organization, and I apparently lacked the people skills to redirect the group. Toward the end of my term late in 2014, while I was wondering if I could add *any* value to the club during my tenure, I had the idea of developing a book. Under the label of Wood Islands Prints I had published two books of my own and some 20 books for other local authors and groups, including three for the Montague Library Writers Guild. Hearing that the Senior Secretariat offered a grant program to underwrite projects that would involve and enhance the experiences of seniors on the Island, I submitted a proposal to develop a book of memories and we won a grant sufficient to pay the cost of printing a several-hundred-copy run of books, to provide free contributor copies and to cover a few incidental expenses. [Thank–you to The Senior Secretariat, the government agency that so honoured our efforts.]

All around me are seniors who have an immense wealth of memories that will gradually be lost as they pass away; how we need to capture these memories for posterity!

I quickly discovered that my expectation of club members all turning in electronic files of their contributions would not fly. Most seniors are shy around computers and uncomfortable on a typewriter—they apparently feel any writing that goes onto paper must be in some way 'literary'. A few folks provided handwritten pieces, but it was not nearly enough material. Finally I stumbled on the key—group audio recordings. I had used a bit of the grant funds purchasing a tiny audio recorder in hopes that individual members would take them to shut-ins and bring back their oral stories, but when we began inviting members to come together and share memories the situation changed. Group recordings were surprisingly successful. We would gather—usually 3 to 6 of us in a circle—and start off with my saying something like, "This week let's talk about how you did laundry when you were growing up." Being in groups—as the first person recounted a story, someone else would be inspired to chime in with a similar experience, and the shyness evaporated. Hearing about the 'old guys' sitting over their coffees at Tim's [Tim Horton's] swapping yarns, I should have recognized this sooner. The entire shape of the book changed. Instead of carefully-crafted stories, we would present off-the-cuff verbatim conversations. The completion was delayed by the difficulty in finding persons or means to transcribe the recordings—apparently all dictation secretaries of the past are either holding out for more pay, too busy, or deceased. Aside from a little help from Barbara Wright-Mackenzie and Marie MacIntyre, I ended up doing all the transcription work myself. I put it off, hunting for help for about a year, but in the end I discovered a free on-line voice-recognition program, '*dictation.io*' which could provide me a flawed, rough draft in digital format. I would listen to the recorded audio in headphones and simultaneously repeat it back into my computer's microphones. I then had to go back through each rough piece, correcting the recognition errors and identifying the speakers. Well over half of the pieces in this book are verbatim or slightly edited printouts of those conversations. Most conversations have been partitioned and arranged by topic—even written pieces with a single contributor are so arranged. The group sessions appear exactly the way the conversation progressed (until it wandered off to another topic) with brief holes where too many people began talking at the same time or were too far off-microphone to be deciphered. There were three written, mixed-topic pieces submitted, that have been separated into smaller, single-topic pieces and arranged with other pieces on the same topic. The table of contents lists all the topics and titles for the individual pieces. If you wish to read, for example, various contributions reminiscing about experiences doing the wash, you can go directly to that section.

CAST OF CHARACTERS (CONTRIBUTORS)

Rather than using the full name of each contributor over and over, I list here, alphabetically, the first names used for identification in the pieces, beside their full names. Thank-you to all of you who contributed.

Arlene	Arlene MacQueen
Barb	Barb Jones
Barbara	Barbara Wright-MacKenzie
Corena	Corena Gairns
Donald	Donald Nicholson
Donna	Donna Munroe
Dora	Dora MacKenzie
Ethel	Ethel Nicholson
Helen	Helen Martell
Ida	Ida MacKenzie (nee Collier)
dd	Isabel Nicholson (nee Buell)
Louise	Louise Burley
Mary	Mary Angela White
Mary Ellen	Mary Ellen MacKinnon
Miriam	Miriam Nicholson
Neil	Neil Brydon
Pat	Pat Wheatley
Peggy	Peggy McDonald
Rhonda	Rhonda McLeod
Richard	Richard Praught
Ron	Ron Ramsey
Ruth	Ruth Nicholson (nee Campbell)
Therese	(Sister) Therese MacDonald
Tina	Tina Fournier
Tom	Thomas Schultz
Veda	Veda Duvar
Winnie	Winifred McCormick

TABLE OF CONTENTS

Introduction 1

Childhood/Parenting 2
   Marriage and Babies 2
      Babies 2
      Premature Childbirth 2
      Frequent Babies 2
      Work before play 3
      Mischief 3
      Casual parenting 4
      More on parents 5
      Married life and babies 5
      Hopped in the car 7
      Arguments and finances 7
   Play 7
      Funerals and Plays 7
      My horse 8
      All summer at the beach 8
      Day at the lake 9
   Chores 10
      No training 10
      Hens tasted the water 11
   Other Early Memories 12
      Washtub bath outside 12
      Hair curling 12
      Two or three to a bed 12
      Spell it 13

School 14
   Walking to school 14
      Stick in the box 14
      School 15
      Sitting in wet clothes 15
      Home for lunch 16
   Teachers & methods 16
      Drafted to teach 16
      Left Handed 17
      Meals to school 17
      Drawing my lessons 18

Reading and memorizing 19
  Poetry, books, and math 19
Other school experiences 21
  School Sports 21

Seasons and weather 22
Fall 22
  Harvesting and butchering 22
  Nor'easter 22
  Winter travel 22
  Deep Snow 23
  Above his head 23
  Snowbound 24
  Sitting on the rim 24
  Ice skating 25
Spring 26
  Maple syrup bath 26
  Rescued off the bridge 26
  Saskatchewan floods and fires 28
Summer 30
  Lightning 30
  Lightning rods 31
  Whitewash 33
  Eye of the hurricane 33

Activities 40
Church/Sundays 40
  I heard every word you sang 40
  Our church 40
  Dad and Ministers 42
  Getting ready 43
  Walking to church 43
  Sunday afternoons 43
  Catholicism and Fundamentalism 43
  Prayer to St. Therese 46
  Hillcrest Gospel Singers Songbook] 47
Going to town 48
  Dances in Montague 48
  Dances all the time 48
  Activities 49
Birthdays 49
  Premier birthday party 49
  Toughest cake 50
  Topped with 50 candles 52
  Flamingos on the lawn 53

First birthday cakes 54
Libraries & Reading 55
   The joy of our local library 55
   Finally allowed to go 56
   Going by bicycle 57
   Her nose in a book 58
Old Home Week 59
   The Provincial Exhibition 59
   A perfect loaf 61
   Picking for admission 61
   Horse racing 61
   Rides and potato picking 62
Fairs 64
   Antique machinery shows 64
   Royal (Toronto) Winter Fair 65
   Away to skating contests 67

Holidays 68
Halloween 68
   Trick or treating 68
   Ghost arising in the cemetery 70
   Creating a haunted house legend 70
   Bump in the night 73
Christmas 73
   Homemade decorations 73
   Presents 74
   Stockings 74
   Santa Claus, presents, and kindness 74
   School Christmas concert 76
   Tree for the kittens 76
Easter 77
   Holy Week for a Catholic 77
Canada Day 79
   Origins 79
   True North 81

Memorable Events 83
Wars 83
   Knitting for the troops 83
   War evacuee to Canada 83
   War brides 85
   German doctor 86
   Blackouts 86
Disasters 87
   Chimney fire 87

Seeing the Hindenburg 88
Elections 92
　Honest politicians 92
　Election day 92
　Political parties and Confederation 93

Transportation 95
Horses 95
　Jack the triumphant horse 95
　Hitching up the horse 97
　Taking the reins 97
　Going for a horse & buggy ride 97
Motor Vehicles 98
　First vehicle 98
　Old (British) cars 98
　Never a driver's license 99
　Licenses for everyone 100
　Road feel 100
　Antique trucks 101
　A new Model T 103
　Cat Under the Hood 105
Ferries 106
　Georgetown ferry 106
　Train crossing on the ferry 107
Trains 107
　Walking was faster 107
　Backing up 108
　Near miss 110
　Trip to Toronto 110
　Riding among soldiers 111

Advertising Slogans 113
　Tiger in the tank 113

Utilities 114
Houses 114
　Moving by horses 114
　Building from scratch 114
Heating 115
　Winterizing 115
　Out in the snow 116
Electricity 116
　Arrival of Electricity 116
　Shock in the tub 118
Plumbing: in and out 119

    Wells 119
    Outhouse blew over 119
    Outhouse burned down 119
    Indoor plumbing 120
    Outhouse at school 121
    Water heater problems 121
Telephones 123
    In the early days 123
    Party lines 124
    Waiting for the line 125
    Party line (dis)courtesy 125
    Operators 126
    Operators I've known 127
    "No Its My Baby" 127
    Later Phones 128

Family memories 130
    Third of eight 130
    Reunited 130
    Second youngest of eight 130
    Deaf sister 131
    Having our picture taken 131
    Seamstress 131
    My father 132
    A martyr is my relative 132
People I Remember 133
    My Friend Mrs. Lem 133
    Grammie MacKenzie 136

Entertainment 137
Radio and TV 137
    Our first radio 137
    Battery conflict 137
    Radio programs 137
    More radio programs 138
    Halls of Ivy 139
    Hockey and the mouse 140
    First sight of a TV 140
    TV and the loss of innocence 141
Music 142
    Family music times 142
    Kids in the background 142
    Dancing 142
    Never too old to learn 143
Other entertainment 144

xi

    Across the ice to the movies 144
    Disneyland roller coaster 144
    Comics and wishes 145

Work & jobs 146
Farming 146
Farm tasks 146
Automated Churn 146
Milking and milk processing 147
Brief butter business 148
Cream, butter and a ploughing match 149
Ice cream and hail 150
Dairy farming and creameries 150
Milking 152
Farm jobs 153
Crops 154
Experiences in barns 156
More on hand milking 157
Farm machinery 159
Antique farm equipment 161
Sugar beets 161
Harvest meals at grandmother's 163
Volunteering to help neighbours 165
Harvesting 166
Fishing 167
Packing herring 167
Boating jobs 168
Other jobs 169
Cordwood 169
Women's Lib 169
Lighthouse keeper 169
Cashier 171
Leaving for work 174
The Depression Years 174
First time to Ontario 175
Returning to the Island 176
Seizing the time 176
Moving to PEI 177
Yankees from the States 178

Medicine 180
Doctors 180
Country doctor 180
Doctor as dentist 180
Secretly removing a scar 181

    Illnesses and diseases 183
        I fight polio 183
        Snowmobile trip for appendicitis 185

Self-sufficiency 187
    Laundry and clothes 187
        Clothes barrel treasures 187
        Beating rugs 187
        Scrub board 188
        Arm in the wringer 188
        Wringer washer 189
        Monday is wash day 191
        Wash/electrification 191
    Winter survival 192
        Food in the cellars 192
        Stocked up for winter 192
    Gardening 193
        Big gardens to weed 193
        Mom's baking 193
        What did your mother say? 193
    Care for the elderly 194
        Taking in relatives 194
        Nana as family 195
        Let me die in peace 196

Landmarks 197
    Buildings 197
        Museum, caskets, and dry goods 197
        Credit union and egg grading 200

Aging 202
    How time passes 202
        It creeps up 202
        Things look too big 203
        New door opening 204
        Aging 204
        Dancing with Jake 205
        Cultivating friendship 208

50+ club 210
    Purpose 210
    Origins 210

INTRODUCTION

Tom Schultz [Editor]: I begin with the front section of a wonderful piece which Mary Angela White put together from a recorded tea party she had with her friends, Dora MacKenzie and Arlene MacQueen. She titled it "Three 'From Away'." She has given me permission to distribute pieces of her lengthy contribution, but I begin here with her lead-in, which inspired the cover picture. I wish I could have been there, sitting around her coffee table, sharing biscuits and tea! Here begins Mary's account:

Mary: The sun was pouring through the wide windows of the sunny back room, windows that showed the white snow drifts that still covered the back yard. It was early May, 2015, and the area was recovering from the persistent white winter that had plagued PEI. We each sat in a comfortable recliner with tea and biscuits set out for us on a low wooden coffee table.

I was recording Dora and Arlene's stories while we all sipped tea and reflected on our early memories. All three of us had come to the Island through marriage. Dora to Hanford MacKenzie of Belfast, Arlene to Don MacQueen originally from Wood Islands, and myself when my daughter Kate had followed Jonathan Costain back from college in Truro; he was from O'Leary, and they invited me along when I retired. Dora is a tiny lady, her hair perfectly curled and her clothes coordinated shades of blue. Arlene is also petite, her once red hair now quite white and her face lined with laughter. Her eyes are bright blue, eager for life and living.

Dora: I was the youngest of a family of fifteen, four brothers and eleven sisters. I wonder sometimes how my parents ever managed to provide for us. I was born in Summerville (N.S.). It's about 20 or 25 miles from Windsor.

Arlene: So the same (distance) as from Montague to here, [said her dear friend Arlene MacQueen, as we sat in her cozy sunroom in Belfast]

Dora: Oh no, less.

Dora: My father, John Coleman Kirby Munroe, worked on the little ferry boat.

[The rest of this lengthy session has been partitioned by topic and distributed throughout this book.]

CHILDHOOD/PARENTING

MARRIAGE AND BABIES

Babies

[Dora had written out her thoughts on the past and referred to them now.]

Dora: When I was born (1929) they thought I was dead. So they put me over on the couch—my sisters tell me this too—I was supposed to be dead — and left me and worked on my mother. I was the last one to be born; I don't know how old she was when I was born. They heard a whimper and it was me! And then they said I was fed with an eye-dropper. So I must have been a tough old bird because I'm here!"

[We laughed, 'tough old bird' being far from how we thought of Dora.]

Premature Childbirth

Veda: I was born in 1935 in April—April 27th and we still had a lot of snow, and our road wasn't paved so it wasn't cleared off in the winter time. When my mother went into premature labour, they called the local midwife and she came, and they also called the doctor from Charlottetown. My father left home to go down to the pavement which was two and a half miles away, to meet the doctor and bring him up. Anyway, when he got there, I had already been born. Now I weighed 3 pounds 6 ounces. They kept me warm on the oven door, and I was fed with an eyedropper. Needless to say it was successful because I'm still here at 82—or almost 82, no, 81.

Frequent Babies

Arlene: Well, back then—Ray came from a family of ten. And you know, the girls went to the States and they'd send money back to their families."

Dora: Ida and John lived in Panama. For all their married life—and then they settled in Florida. And Ida—they told me, everybody had a baby to look after in the family because every two years you'd have a baby. So I looked after me, apparently.

Mary: Now, wasn't that smart. Soon as the kids get old enough, "OK. This one's yours." Two years later, the next youngest...

Dora and Arlene: Yes!

Dora: Everybody had one to look after. She was organized, my mother was.

Work before play

Peggy (McDonald): We didn't live like we do today—we worked—just three sisters. That was the way we lived. We always had to work all the time. We done work with my father—inside and out—we worked with the wood and the cows and the horses and the sheep. We worked with them all. We walked every place—to the post office. We went to church with the horse and wagon.

If we had time to play.... We did our own thing, like, when we were kids. We had no toys. We had no nothing. We just done our own whatever. We rode horse back, we rode cow's back, we rode sheep's back, and we done everything. We made our own fun of anything we wanted, we made it ourselves to play with. I never had a doll or anything like that in my life. My sister had one, but I used to be home from school a lot because I was I was sick and when she was away I'd have her doll—I'd play with the doll—make clothes for it and put her back in her bed before she come home. You know, it's just like that—it's different than today. We never had anything going on.

Mischief

Tina: Did you have any special things that happened as you were growing up other than that?

Peggy: Not really, just sports. We used to play against other schools and stuff like that. Nothing really special. Just the way we lived—we were quite pleased. We thought we had a great time. We had nothing to play with but we did our own thing.

Tina: You made your own toys.

Peggy: We had our own time and everything was good. I wasn't much to sleep. We didn't have electricity just the old kerosene lamps. When night came the lamps were put out and you went to bed, but I never used to sleep much. I used to think what I was going do the next day—good or not.

Tina: Did you get into mischief?

Peggy: Oh yeah.

Tina: How's about giving me some mischief.

Peggy: I used to get into mischief and then my mother would lock me in the bedroom, for a while, and I'd be sitting in there with nothing to play with. I'd be sittin' in there thinking about of what I was going to do when I get out. If anybody said things you weren't supposed to do, I would try them—I'd have to do it—find out what it was like. If the people in at night like, I said playing cards and that, they'd be talking—they all talked Gaelic but they didn't spoke English a lot, but we knew all the Gaelic and the conversation was about everything in the neighbourhood—everything that went on, good or bad. I used hear it all—they didn't think I understood. I'd know it all and when I'd get back to school after I be sick, the kids would sit around I'd be telling them all those stories, about everything in the neighbourhood. There was no other way getting news any other way. We thought it was a great life.

Tina: We all enjoyed our lives. They were more simple than today.

Peggy: You were never bored. There was always something to do, but you did it yourself. Like I say we had our work to do but then we had time to play.

Casual parenting

Mary: Mom was not very motherly. When they got married, she would have been 32 and he was 40. She had gone to Ottawa to work during the war, and then in 1948 or '49 she came home and married Dad.

Arlene: They were older then.

Mary: Yes. So Mom's idea of parenting was 'the sun's out, go outdoors.' So we were outdoors every morning, every afternoon and every evening 'til dark. I think she was overwhelmed because she had 8 children and two or three miscarriages between 1950 and 1962. So just keeping the wash done, and doing the dishes and cooking meals was all she could handle.

Dora: And they didn't have all the conveniences either.

More on parents

Arlene: The women didn't have it easy. In those days, they had nothing to work with. You heated your place with wood, and you cooked.

Dora: Ida always used to tell me I was a gabby little thing. She told me one time not to tell anybody, something not to tell in front of Mom, and I came right out and told them, 'Oh, yes, I know, I know,' and told on somebody.

Arlene: My Dad used to sail, that was before they joined up in the First World War. And there was a big storm that came up on Lake Huron and they lost a lot of ships. But the captain made for shore into a little cove and they were saved.

And we, my brother and my sister, used to razz him 'If the captain hadn't done that, we wouldn't be here!'

Married life and babies

Arlene: How old were you [Mary] when you got married?

Mary: Twenty. Yup, thought we knew it all. [sighed]

Arlene: I was a few days off 21. Ray wanted to get married when I was 18.

Dora: I didn't have two clues when I got married. I thought it was gonna be like heaven. [laughter more raucous this time, three of us in unison.] It was a rude awakening. You soon smarten up.

Arlene: Oh, you grow up.

Dora: Well, I was 18 and Ray wanted to get married. The company was sending him out to B.C. and I said, "No, but if you ask me in two years, I'll reconsider."

Mary: Weren't you ahead of your time!

Dora: And he went out west and he wrote to me every week and he phoned me and then when he came back, in two years, and he came up to Kincardine, and we got engaged."

Mary: Did he bring a ring with him?

Dora: No, we went and picked it and in three weeks I got married. Mom thought I was absolutely crazy.

Mary: But you had this on the back burner for two years!

Dora: Yes. But I went out with other guys and I had a good time. I thought he'd go out west and find somebody else. I just assumed that.

I couldn't wait to have a baby after I got married.

Mary: Well you came from a big family.

Arlene: Yes, this is it, you did.

Dora: That was the thing. To get married and have a baby. I was married in '47. And Barbara was born the next year at Christmas time, the 19th. Didn't take me long to get pregnant. Barbara often figured it out to see if I had to get married. [She had to talk over the laughter this time.] I got married in '47 and she wasn't born 'til '48, the next year. So I passed. I never thought of doing anything like that with my mother, never thought of it.

Mary: But kids do now. My parents were married the end of December and my brother was born in July. It doesn't quite add up.

Arlene: That's all right. Things aren't going to change. It happens.

Dora: And at those times, you didn't plan your children, or you didn't plan to get pregnant.

Arlene: Oh, good lord, no.

Dora: And there were accidents—you weren't planning. If it happens, it happens.

Arlene: I wasn't supposed to be. She [my mother] had the two children and then she lost two. And that's why there's a gap. And she didn't want any more. And then I came along.

Dora: Every eighteen months or two years, there was one in our family.

Arlene: Yes, every two years.

Mary: That's because the breast feeding would die off. Around a year old and then she would get pregnant. Things were different.

Dora: But we were happy. I think people were more happy then, than they are today. We were happy, didn't want anything 'cause we knew we couldn't have anything.

Arlene: [sadly] It's much different today.

We had second-hand clothes—my brothers were out working and I'd write to them and ask for the catalogue.

You'd buy a coat for $7.95 or even a jacket for $5.95. And Art, Eddy and Donny were all working —and they'd give me money because they were working on the gypsum boats.

Hopped in the car

dd: I met my husband-to-be in Murray River. My sister and I were walking on the street, and their car stopped and we talked to them and we got in. It was 1947. They were Mack Nicholson and Athol Dewar. I married Mack in November 1948, and we had six children.

Arguments and finances

Dora: We've all had a pretty good life, I'd say. "Well I've never known violence," I remarked.

Dora: No, I never did either.

Arlene: I didn't either. In fact, long after I was married, I asked Mom, I said 'Did you and Dad ever have an argument?' and she said 'Everyone always has an argument. But we did it when you kids were in bed. And we did it quietly.' Because I never heard them say a nasty word to each other."

Dora: I never heard anything like that. And another thing, we never heard anything about financial."

Arlene: No, we didn't either.

Mary: I can remember Mom saying something about needing more money for groceries. And she started cutting the milk with powdered milk. And I think that's why my teeth are so bad! Because I had them all out when I was 13—all the top ones.

PLAY

Funerals and Plays

Corena: You talk about playing. We used to have—kind of morbid—we used to have funerals for—we had these baby chickens, and when one of them died or whatever, we would put the body in a strawberry box [laughter], and we would have a little funeral, and this guy that lived down the road from me, he said we should sing *Bringing In The Sheaves.* One time I remember my brother started to laugh. He [the neighbour boy] was quite annoyed at him and told him, "That isn't what to do at a funeral. You're supposed to be crying—not laughing." He chastised him for the laughing.

That's what we did as kids. We also used to put plays on. You can imagine the plays. And invite the neighbours to come. We made our own plot, I guess. Who wrote—I don't remember all the details, but these are some of the things we did as children.

Tom: Did you charge for tickets?

Corena: No [laughing], I don't think we charged. We were just pleading with neighbours to come to see it. [still laughing] We didn't charge. Years later I took part in plays, but anyway.... No, in those years we didn't charge.

My horse

Barbara: Once upon a time long ago and far away there was a little girl who lived on a farm. Her favourite animals on the farm were those you would usually find, and her favourite one was her horse.

All summer at the beach

Tom: Okay, we're talking about how it was in terms of being so close to the shore on PEI and what you did as a kid.

Pat: Well of course we lived on the North River Road and our farm was both sides of the road and so we would wander down and through the cattle and to the beach and that's usually where we spent most of the summer when we weren't doing Farm chores. A lot of the neighbours' kids were about our age and we'd all go down. We all learnt to swim from one another—I don't think any of us ever took lessons. Nobody came down to see if we were all right. We just wandered down and spent the afternoon. We used to dig clams, and we would have an old sheet of iron and we would make a little fire and we would put these clams on the iron and we would open them and just eat them right out of the shell.

One day my sister and I decided the tide was well out and we would walk across the North River to Beech Grove. It looked quite close. So we waded in and off we went. Well, we were slogging across—actually it was very muddy and the further we got the muddier it got. Well we're almost up to our knees in mud, and she said, "I don't think we're any closer to Beach Grove than we were when we started. So anyway, one thing and another, we kept slogging, but then I felt I had hurt my foot. I hauled it up out of the mud and I had gashed it on one of those razor clams and it was about it 3 inch gash and it was bl-e-e-ding all over the place. So we decided to give up our trek over to Beach Grove and we had to turn around and come back—didn't dare say anything to Mother, so we just kind of packed it with the dirt. It eventually stopped bleeding. I never suffered any ill-effects. Basically that's what we did all summer. We hung out at the beach. It was a great time. This was '40... '45 during the war years when I was evacuated here. It just seemed blissful to me because, having grown up in London, England, we never saw the beach—didn't see many trees either. This was just the most idyllic place—hated to leave.

Tom: Did they get mosquitoes down there?

Pat: Oh yes, there's mosquitoes everywhere isn't there? We always said the black flies came first when the leaves were opening and after black flies left, the first of August, the mosquitoes moved in. It was just like one of those preordained things.

Tom: Did you have bug-repellent or anything or did you just get bit?

Pat: I guess we just got bitten. I never thought about it until you mentioned it. We'd never heard of bug-repellent in those days. Maybe we were so scruffy the bugs didn't bother with us.

Tom: Too much dirt! They couldn't get in.

Pat: That's right.

Day at the lake

Richard: Previous to us owning a motor vehicle, there was a lake about 3 miles in back called O'Keefe's Lake. Doesn't ring a bell? It's a freshwater lake. In those days there was entertainment and a canteen. That was our highlight of a Sunday afternoon. All of us—my four sisters and neighbour's family—would all get on the horse and truck wagon and we would all head for O'Keefe's Lake. This road that we took to O'Keefe's Lake was just a wagon road. There was no cars went through it and there was a lot of deep holes and all that stuff. So we'd leave home at 1 o'clock and we'd take off through this road with this single horse and we'd swim and then we'd head for home. On one occasion we had a smaller wagon they called a driving wagon, and we get into one of the bad holes and the horse went right out of the shafts. So there we were with the wagon stuck and the horse out of the shafts and the harness all broke. So we hada get the wagon out and the harness patched up to go home. But it was quite an occasion.

Pat: At the lake?

Richard: At O'Keefe's Lake. When we got the motor vehicles, my father used to take us to the beaches. We went to Cavendish Beach and we went to Panmure Island and whatever other beaches, and of course we still went to O'Keefe's Lake. I learnt to swim—don't ask me how—but I could swim.

[?]: Most of us could

Richard We enjoyed the fresh water. That was a fresh water lake. It's still there and they still swim in it.

Ron: We swam, and basically that was it.

Tom: You swam and that was it?

Ron: We swam. We played in the sand. There was 8 of us in the family. Cover all they used to call it back then.

Tom: So you never lacked for companions.

CHORES

No training

Mary: And I was the oldest girl. We would have company and they'd say, 'Oh, you have these lovely girls, I'm sure they're a big help,' but she never let us help her. I didn't learn much about housework until I started, in grade 9, being a mother's helper. It was from the lady I worked for that I learned how to cook, to clean, and to iron.

[My parents] had got a vacuum cleaner and I volunteered to vacuum the upstairs every week for a quarter. And she kinda laughed like, 'That'll never happen,' and that became my weekly chore.

I always thought, 'I should be helping,' but didn't know what to do. One time, I offered to hang the clothes out because there were always clothes to be hung out, with seven of us. So I diligently went out and pinned everything on the clothesline and I ran out of clothespins. So I went in, 'Mom, are there any more clothes pins?'

'What do you mean—there are lots of clothes pins.' She came out and looked at the line and said, 'Well you're supposed to hook them together, not two clothes pins to every piece!' and I said, 'How am I supposed to know?!' and I ran back in the house and never did it again.

We could have been such a help to her. My sister Bernadette was just a year and a half younger than me and we could have been a big help.

Arlene: Because that's what you do. You get your kids to help you.

Dora: Every Saturday evening, I'd scrub the kitchen floor. We'd have to scrub it and wax it with the old hard wax and, to shine it, we'd pull each other across the floor. You had to have it just shiny or my mother would make you do it all over again, just like that.

We'd work all day if we were home. Everything had to be done or you wouldn't get out to play.

Arlene: Oh yeah, your jobs had to be done. Mom didn't like us to help her cook. So when I got married, we went out to B.C. and the first meal I made, Ray started to laugh. 'What are you laughing about?' and he said, 'I knew what I was going to get for supper because your Mom told me it was the only thing you knew how to make.' It was meat loaf and scalloped potatoes. [Laughter]

She'd get me to do housework but not help with the cooking. So when I got married, I didn't know how to cook. And that suited me fine. I'd help Dad and I'd always cut the lawn and there was a lot of lawn. Not like today, I'd have to push it—and when you're by the water, you're on a slant all the time.

Hens tasted the water

Corena: They had potatoes. There was people at our place and they were picking potatoes, and I wasn't very old. They sent me to the house to get some water.

I took a long time before I came back, and they said, "Where were you?"

I said, "Well I went to get under the fence and the hens came and tasted the water so I had to spill that out and go back."

I must have had a small bucket or something, but I told them the hens had tasted the water so I had to take it back and pump—brought more water for them.

OTHER EARLY MEMORIES

Washtub bath outside

Ethel: I remember in the 1930's my Mom giving my sister and me a bath outside in our yard on a hot sunny day in her washtub—age 5 or 6 or perhaps younger.

Hair curling

Dora: I remember my sister, Lorena, and I, we would be curling each other's hair with the kerosene lamps. We'd place the tongs in the glow of the lamp. I can still smell her hair sizzling. Sometimes, we'd put our hair up in rags. Where there's a will, there's a way. But we had a great time.

Two or three to a bed

Dora: We never had our own bedroom; there was always a double bed plus a single bed in the room. Do you remember the song '*Sticking Your Gum on*

Childhood/Parenting: Other Early Memories

the Bedpost Overnight? Well that was what we usually did, but it was usually spruce gum."

Mary: How many to a bed?

Dora: There'd be two to a bed, sometimes three. In my time, see, my nieces were almost the same age as me. My older sister, Carrie, had family the same age as I was, almost.

So if they came to visit, they stayed all night, so they slept there, too.

Spell it

Dora: Oh, I didn't put in about moving to Windsor. I was about 12 years old when we moved to Windsor.

We didn't have electricity and we had a battery operated radio we turned on for the news, *Don Messer and the Islanders,* plus boxing matches Saturday night. I remember my father reading the paper with a kerosene lamp. We'd be doing our homework and I'd be asking my father 'What does this mean, Pup?' I shouldn't say 'Pup' but that's what we always called him.

He would say 'Spell it.' then I'd write down the meaning. He'd just continue reading with his glasses halfway down his nose. He'd read every page of the paper.

My father was an engineer on the little ferry Rotundus. It went by, according to the tides, from Summerville to Hantsport, Avondale, and Windsor every day. I would watch for him and go to meet him. He always had a peppermint in his pocket or a bite of his sandwich for me.

SCHOOL

WALKING TO SCHOOL

Stick in the box

Corena: I have a little story about going to school. The school was—the building is gone now—the school that I attended first was right next to where our Lower Montague cemetery is. Anyway I started school when I was five. I had my birthday in May. Mom went... yes, they would let me go. They weren't that strict and I wanted to go. Anyway, I had a friend who lives up the road from me and I would—so she said to come with her. She was older than I by a year or year-and-a-half. Anyway she had already started school. So off I went, and she had a lane—not too long, with a mailbox at the end of the road— she said that, if she had left for school, she would put a stick in the box just so I would know not to go up her lane. So this had never happened until one day I went, and the stick was in the box. I was very upset. Five years old and have to walk to school by myself. So I go past the local store and the man who owned the store, Raymond Poole came out and asked me what was the matter, and he told my

mother later, he said, "I couldn't make head nor tail of the child all. All she kept saying was, 'there was a stick in the box'." He was kind enough to take me and drive me to school. So Mom later told this story because she sure got a kick out of it. She knew what had taken place.

School

Miriam: I went to a one-room school and had the same teacher, Annie MacPherson, for six years. I remember her taking some of us home at noon in her car. We would sit out on the front of the house and eat our lunch. We walked to school, but in the winter we were driven by horse sleigh.

Sitting in wet clothes

Mary Ellen: We had cows which had to be milked before going to school.

During the winter Mom would cook Cream of Wheat and porridge to be ready to heat up in the morning or at night before bed.

We walked a mile to school. Mom knitted mittens and socks for us to wear. We wore clothes given to us, and we were glad to get them. I remember times when the snow was up to our bellies and we would arrive at the school only to find the fire wasn't on. The neighbour near the school was in charge, but many times he would fail to have it lit. We would have to sit in wet clothes all day and walk home that way.

There were 8 grades in the one-room schoolhouse. Lunch for school consisted of home-made bread or biscuits with molasses. At lunch time we might have a game of baseball or play hopscotch or hide-and-seek. [Once a year at school] there would be a day of playing, including the 2-leg race. Fudge was made to raise money for school books. This was a picnic.

Home for lunch

Dora: That's a great cup of tea. [At this point, Arlene's son Doug arrived to replenish our tea and serve us cake. Conversation turned to our schooling.]

Mary: We were a 20 minute walk from school.

Arlene: Well, everybody walked. Anywhere you wanted to go, you walked. And there were no buses, either.

Mary: And we came home at lunch. Jam sandwich. We were home for about 10 minutes, turned around and went back to school. We were still in town and you had to be outside of town limits to get a bus. So we walked.

Dora: You had a lot of fun, I bet, walking to school with all the kids, did you?

Mary: There was usually one girl I would walk back and forth with.

Arlene: We didn't have to be back to school 'til 1:30—got out at 12:00. Everybody walked. A lot of the girls I knew, they had further to go than I did. But everybody walked.

Mary: So did you go 'til grade 12?

Arlene: No, 11. Then I quit.

Teachers & methods

Drafted to teach

Tina: You mentioned the fact that you had been a teacher—you were a teacher?

Peggy: Yeah. I had no notion of being a teacher, but when I finished grade 11, the teacher of our school left at Christmas, and she didn't come back, so the trustees came to the house. My father was [asked?] for me to go and teach. I had no notion I would teach in school, 'cause I wasn't good in school, but I went and I did it for them 'cause they wanted me—grade 1 to grade 6 then. And I did school. And then Dad said 'cause I filled in for them, next school year I could teach [the whole year]. So I did for another year, and then I went to teach school in Glen Cove which was a-w-a-a-y back in the woods. In those days you didn't go to the store or anywhere in the winter. You took in all your food in the fall and everything. I stayed at my cousin's—there was four kids in school—two boys and two girls—grades four and five—that's all there was at the school. I taught school there and then, next year I started out at the school in Mabel[?]. It was a bigger school, but my sister got sick—she took polio and went to Halifax. She wanted me to go, so I went. That ended my teaching, of which I had no notion of ever doing, but I ended up doin' it.

Left Handed

dd: The first day in school, I'm left handed. The teacher used to make me use my right hand. And he hit me across the knuckles with his ruler. My Mom took me to the doctor and he said, "She is completely left handed. Don't try to change it." The doctor gave my Mom a note for the teacher.

Meals to school

Corena: I could remember parents in the community—this was in lower Montague—used to take a meal for all the children at the school. I'm not sure how often they did it—maybe once a month—I'm not certain on that aspect of it. Anyway, they would do that 'cause I remember Mom used to make a casserole that I still make—it's one of my comfort foods. It's macaroni, and hamburger, and stewed tomatoes. You mixed all that up and cooked it—a good sized casserole. She would have to make a couple—I don't remember how many students there were at the school. When it was Mom's turn I remember Mom—that's what she would make—these casseroles. Then

Dad would make a small freezer of homemade ice cream.

[general comment]: Wow.

Corena: I also remember another woman who lived down the road. They had a big boarding house or maybe like a hotel or something, where people stayed. She used to make like the chocolate cake with a seven-minute icing. Sometimes her sons brought that to school—the other boys would be trying to trade to see if they could get some of this. When it was her turn, that's what she made for dessert—I don't remember the main course. Also our teacher used to cook things at the school.

Okay I'd be almost ready to leave home and then I'd say to Mom, "Oh, I have to bring a turnip" or "I have to bring carrots." She'd be making a pot of soup but she did that. At the school we had some dishes and cups and I can remember this cupboard and that's what was in it

[?]: In Georgetown?

Corena: No, Lower Montague, at the Lower Montague School. We did it—how often I'm not sure. I'd say to Mom, "I have to bring this or that."

Drawing my lessons

Peggy: We went to school. The school was near our place and everybody was in one class. Everybody walked there—there was no buses then or anything.

Tina: You had also said something about drawing your pictures instead of writing down what was on the blackboard?

Peggy: Oh yes, I didn't like writin'—I didn't like school—doing anything in school, but I liked drawing. At night I used to draw—I'd be at home from school a lot, and my other sister could be in bed, and there'd be people in—they'd be playing cards. There was no Tim Horton's or anything—they visited one another. I'd be down on the floor. I had a piece of birch bark— you can draw pictures on the birch bark—the inside of it.

One day we had to write a composition about—it was poems, and I didn't like poems—*Elegy Written in a Country Churchyard,* and I wouldn't write it. I went home and I drew a picture of a man sittin' down writing, and all the tombstones on the ground, and everything like that, and [the other children] were all saying to me, "You're gonna be a goner because you didn't do your homework." I gave it to her—she took it and she put it up on the wall. It was good; she liked it. So I could draw all the time.

READING AND MEMORIZING

Poetry, books, and math

Winnie: I went to a one-room school. I was lucky; I had the same teacher for five-six years. There was 28 or 30 children from grade 1 through grade 10.

Tom: One teacher?

Winnie: One teacher. She taught all the subjects. She put the math problems for the younger grades on the board the evening before. The students had to copy them down into their scribblers, and do them, and while they were doing that, she could tend to some of the older children. In grade 3 you had to do memory work: poetry and the times table. We had to stand up in a row and recite whatever poem we were doing at the time.

Tom: Do you still remember any of the poems?

Winnie: Oh yes. *Barefoot Boy with Cheek of Tan*—'with thy rolled up pantaloons and thy merry whistled tunes'.

Tom: 'All too soon these feet must hide within the prison gates of pride'—that's the tail end.

Winnie: 'I was once a barefoot boy' is somewhere in there and 'under the spreading chestnut tree the village smithy stands'... 'his arms are...' 'and the muscles on his brawny arms stood out like (something) trees'. My father took an apprenticeship to become a blacksmith, and the guy that he worked for used to tease him and say, "The muscles on his scrawny arms stood out like sparrows knees."

I loved school, perhaps because as long as you did what you were told, you didn't have to worry—you did your work and nobody bothered you, and the older children had to help the younger ones sometimes. If someone was finished with their work, then they could listen to the younger children do their reading or whatever it was. I couldn't wait to finish my work when I was in, say, grade four or five because the grades seven and eight would read a paragraph from something that they were studying, like *Ichabod*

Crane and the Headless Horseman or *The Ransom of Red Chief,* and I was dying to get finished so I could read the rest of the story. We moved from Rollo Bay to Bear River...

Tom: Where is that?

Winnie: Over on the north side of the Island in Kings County.

Tom: Morell?

Winnie: No, it's further east than Morell.

Tom: I don't get up there much.

Winnie: By that time I was in grade eight or nine, and we had fractions, decimals, and percentage, and I *couldn't* get the connection between these three—it just didn't make any sense to me. I couldn't see it. After my Mom died we moved back to Rollo Bay again, and my uncle was teaching and he put it on the board, and suddenly the light went on! Oh. Okay, now I see. ½ and decimal 5 and 50% is all the same. I loved math from that day to this.

Tom: Were you around here when consolidation started?

Winnie: No, all I remember is my brother and his wife writing and being upset about the fact that their children, who lived in Rollo Bay, were going to have to go to Souris to High School.

OTHER SCHOOL EXPERIENCES

School Sports

Peggy: In school we had track and field and stuff like that. I liked that.

Tina: We had too.

Peggy: We done that all the time. One year my sister was in the over-12 bunch and I was in the under-12 bunch—I was about 10 years old—and we had it [sports day] in Fort Hood, and we done the younger ones in the morning. I was there in the racing and the high jump and the hop-step-jump. I liked them all, and I done them all, and I used to win them. And then my sister couldn't go in because we were jumping off the roof of the barn and she sprained her ankle, and couldn't go, so the teacher got a T-shirt—you went by number not name. Nobody knew you then because you didn't travel anywhere. She got a T-shirt, and they got [my sister's] number and put it on me—put me in with the bigger ones and do the racing and do everything. That was one thing I could do, but when I went over to the high jump and they were doing the little ones, there was a little boy standing there—he wasn't very old—and when I jumped the first time he said, "That one's gonna win. She jumps like [indistinguishable]." And I did. But you know, it's just things like that that are so different than now.

Tina: Oh yeah. We grew up in a different time zone [age].

Peggy: Different time zone altogether.

Seasons and Weather

Fall

Harvesting and butchering

Mary Ellen: Bales of hay had to be loaded on a wagon and stored in the barn loft. We had to stook sheaves of grain. The grain had to be thrashed. Potatoes had to be dug. Dad hired help to get this done. The potatoes had to be graded and stored in the cellar of the house, as well as another building.

Storm windows and doors had to be placed on the house.

Dad and a neighbour would kill a pig. This was pickled in a barrel. We had back bacon and pork shoulders, fished out with a pulp hook. We also had 25 lbs. of salt cod to carry us through the winter.

Mom made potted meat as well as chow, beets, and mustard pickles. We picked cranberries at relatives' houses to do all winter.

Nor'easter

Mary: Well, I suppose living in a lighthouse [on Lake Huron], you'd have to be very aware of the weather.

Arlene: "Oh, yes. See, I love the sound of the wind. When I go to bed, I like the sounds of a nor'easter because I was brought up with that.

Winter travel

Veda: When I was a child, we used to get some really big snow storms—last two or three days—and the snow would be way up—up over the top of the fences and everything...

Tom: You were saying that your road never got ploughed.

Veda: Yeah. Our road didn't get ploughed in the winter time—there was no cars so in the winter time everything was horse and sleigh. We would drive—roads were made across the fields. Fences were either cut, or there was gates there that they could open in the winter time. Sometimes we traveled quite a distance. New Year's Day we always traveled from Winsloe to Crapaud to my aunt's for New Year's Day. We'd have to get up early, early in the morning to get the cows milked and all the farm chores done before we left for the day.

Deep Snow

Mary Ellen: One time we had to go out of the upstairs window and shovel our way to the barn to feed the animals. This took a half-day—the snow was that deep. Back in the '50s the snow was deep. We could almost touch the electric wires. Dozers were out to clear the roads. We couldn't see traffic because of the snow depth, and it would be weeks before the road was cleared. We had to use horse and sleigh to pick people up and take to the store and church. Neighbours were given money and a list in an envelope to pick up groceries, and they would be returned to the owners—you could trust people back then, but not today.

Some times we went coasting on a sleigh. We skated on a pond using skates that attached to our boots. We had no electricity.

We pumped water at the pumphouse and brought in many buckets of water. It was heated by the kitchen stove. Mornings when we got up, before the fire was put on, the water would be frozen in the bucket in the porch.

Above his head

Mary: And I remember a winter like this [winter of 2015], the snow. We lived in a big house next to a ball park and it had a track that was a quarter mile around, so that's how big a field it was. The snow all blew into our driveway. Dad was about 5'8" and Mom has a picture of him out shovelling with my two older brothers and the snow was above his head—they did about half of it and had to come in for a break and then go back out to finish it, it was such a big job.

Snowbound

Miriam: For 2 weeks in a storm, I was in Newtown with 4 of my own children, and 5 of my Brother's. My brother was on a snowplough and he couldn't get home. And we couldn't see the pumphouse because of the drifts. The boys were teenagers then—they had to walk over the bank and down to the pumphouse and haul the water to the house. I made bread and biscuits every day.

Tom: So this was a big storm, I gather.

Miriam: It was 1961. My [sister-in-law] was in the hospital having another baby.

Tom: So how many of you were in the house?

Miriam: 9… 10. Nine children and myself.

Tom: So that was a pretty busy time.

Miriam: Yes.

Tom: And they couldn't go to school because of the snow?

Miriam: That's right. Well, they did after a few days. There'd be one lane though. They'd walk to school.

Tom: OK '61 and they were still traveling by horse?

Miriam: No. No. Well some people still had horse and sleighs.

Tom: The [snow] ploughing was done.

Miriam: The ploughing was done, but the neighbour, two houses up, had to come down. He'd be going by to the store and I'd send down to the store for stuff. There was always plenty of food in the house. There was always canned meat, etc. That was all looked after. We all had our own vegetables.

Sitting on the rim

Tina: In the winter time, Dad would drive us to school. It was half a mile away from where we all lived. He would pick up the neighbours and take them with us. If the snow started getting too heavy, we couldn't go by cars. Then my Dad would shift to the neighbour's grain wagon. He put skis under it for the horses to pull with all of us kids. When the car couldn't go anymore, we picked up 3 *more* kids. Dad put bales of hay in the bottom and quilts so we could cover up. Everything seemed to be working pretty well until the road became impassable even for horses. Then we had to use the field.

One time my father hadn't driven for a while (he would go for two weeks and the other farmers would do their two weeks) and he wasn't exactly sure where the trail was because it was snowed under. He didn't go quite far enough into the field. It was a ploughed field and one of the horses stepped in a hole and it scared him. That horse was the one that only my father could hang on to in the first place. So that horse took off, telling the other horse, "You'd better hurry up or you'll be left behind."

Now my 14 year old brother had a habit of sitting high upon the rim at the corner of the box.

I told him, "Get down with the rest of us," but as soon as I said it, the box tipped and his feet flew up in the air.

He looked really terrified hanging upside down with his head in the snow bank. Some of the boys grabbed one leg, I grabbed the other, and my other brother grabbed him around the back and yanked. He pulled him head over heels back in.

My father looked back, but I said, "Keep on going."

When we got to school I told him if he ever did that again I'd kill him. I didn't care that he was only four—I did not want anybody to go through that anymore.

When we told that to the teacher what had happened he told us, "You guys are lucky but it was just a fluke that happened—it shouldn't have." He never did sit there anymore

Ice skating

Dora: In the winter we skated; we walked a good mile to the pond. Mother put baked potatoes in the toes of our skates to keep them warm. We'd all have to sit down in the snow and ice to put on our skates. We always had a big fire burning at the side. We had lots of fun. There was always a big group of us.

Arlene: In the wintertime, I could go down and we skated. We got snow [by Lake Huron], just like here. And the people are very much like they are here. The town [Kincardine] was 2500 or 3000 people; it was a very pretty town. You walked everywhere. They had a rink where there was skating and hockey. Dad was right into that. He didn't play hockey, but he would never miss a game. There was everything right there, winter or summer, I was busy.

SPRING

Maple syrup bath

Dora: My brother, Arthur, and I would go tap trees, or he'd tap them and I'd be with him. It would be put on the stove, boiling down in a big pot. One day my sister, Minnie Margarette, thought it was water and she bathed my niece Joan in it. That didn't go over too big with my brother. [Arlene and I joined in with her laughter, picturing Art's face.]

Rescued off the bridge

Tom: Tina, you grew up in Alberta, right?

Tina: No, in Manitoba. I have a book on the floods of Manitoba. It's that thick. I have the whole book of Manitoba.

Tom: Stories don't have to be just PEI.

Tina: Unfortunately, I wasn't born and raised on the Island.

Pat: That's a shame—real shame.

Tina: PEI might have been better if I had been here!

Pat: Oh yes, definitely.

Ron: She's 'from away', you know.

Tina: Tell me about it. I met two of my first husband's nieces when they were 16 and in grade 12. They asked me what province I was from and I said, "Manitoba."

"Oh you're from out of—what country are you from?"

"Well," I said, "From Canada."

Seasons and weather: Spring

"Oh no, you can't be. Canada is Ontario and Quebec."

I mean these are grade 12—they're supposed to graduate, and Canada is Ontario and Quebec? We were five years old and we knew what Canada was. These two didn't.

Pat: You know when you live out in British Columbia—I was there for 20 years—and when you're from PEI, they'd say, "Oh that's back east." They lumped everything together. Anything from Montreal was 'back east'. Nobody really gave a thought. We were just sort of the upstarts.

Tina: We were from the dry land.

Tom: I remember we were visiting a church in Massachusetts and we were introduced as people 'from the West'—Indiana is *not* the West, in my view.

Tina: I'm from the West. Going from the East it's the first Western Province: Manitoba, Saskatchewan, Alberta.

Tom: Oh yes, you are going to talk about floods. Did you get floods out there?

Tina: Good heavens—every spring.

Tom: So tell us about the flood in Manitoba.

Tina: I was 10 years old and we were walking to school. And the land—like it's all flat land and there was one little bridge. We walked a mile and a half and then we got to this bridge, then we had to go over that little bridge, and then we walked another half-mile to get to the school. Well, this one day we saw the water. There was water on the land right across—a foot—foot and a half—two feet deep—no big deal. We had been over that bridge. For about a month we had gone over that bridge. The Red River would overflow and the Assiniboine would come in from the US and bring in more water when the snow and ice started to melt. So that's why we always ended up being flooded. We were living 7 miles off the American border. We would get a lot of water. This one morning everybody had gone across. I didn't want to go across. I had two older brothers and the neighbours had two boys that were older than me. There was another boy that was older and a girl that was my age—so they were all across. I wasn't goin' to go across—I was terrified of water, 'cause I'd almost been almost drowned.

So my oldest brother says, "We can't leave you here—can't even let you go home by yourself in case the water goes up. Where would I end up? You've got to come over the bridge. We'll get ahold of the car to get us." It was 10 miles around to get us a mile and a half.

So I said, "Okay." I got two steps onto the bridge—when I hit the third step I screamed! The bridge was going. I'm standing on the middle of the bridge. My oldest brother, he jumped onto the bridge. He didn't care—his life wasn't as important. It was important, but mine was too.

Raymond Berard resides off the Plum River southwest of St. Jean and gets back and forth between home and the outside by boat. Just as many others do. While he had to move his livestock, Berard and his family did not evacuate. (Echo Photo)

Eddie, the neighbour's boy, the older one, he said, "Chain!" As soon as he said, "Chain" everybody grabbed each other's hand and made a chain link. Eddie was the first one next to my brother. My brother grabbed hold of my arm. Eddie still hadn't been able to get close enough to me. He had to be careful. If he went over too far where I was, the bridge with tip. So he had to be careful that he didn't drop both of us into the water. The water was just going like this [gesture not recorded] across the field. We would have kept on going. The water was 3 or 4 feet deep on those fields.

The area around Emerson was getting worse Sunday, April 22 as the mighty Red River flowed over at spots flooding these historical buildings. (Times Photo)

So he looked at me he says, "We've gotta get off of here. We're not going there." We were like, this is the bridge and this is the road [gestures lost]. The bridge was like this. We were on the corner of the road. That's where the bridge stopped. Eddie just gave a yank on me. I didn't let go of his hand. I kept hold of him. So as soon as Eddie got off of the bridge, he swung his other arm over and everybody else grabbed hold of him. He had about four hands on his arm. They just got him. His feet were in the water. So when we got to school they did let one of the neighbours who lived at the other end where there was no water—a little bit of water—not like the amount of water we had walked through—they drove us 10 miles around to get us back to home where we lived and that was a mile and a half that we had to walk. That's my little bridge story.

Saskatchewan floods and fires

Tom: How about flooding? Anybody remember flooding? We don't get really big floods on the Island. Well *you* [Tina] do!

Seasons and weather: Spring

Barbara: It's only Charlottetown that floods now.

Tina: I've got a story but I forgot to bring my book of the Manitoba floods.

Barbara. Well they're still recovering. I went to visit daughter in northern Saskatchewan 2 years ago and we were 7 ½ hours north of Saskatoon which is pretty far north, so we were right up at the border of the tree line. We were coming down to Prince Albert and we drove for I guess a good 3 hours through nothing but scrub on dirt roads and then we struck the pavement and got down onto the plains area, but we'd come to places where you'd see this huge lake and a telephone pole sticking out of the middle of it.

My daughter said, "That was the road, Mom, and still not dried out from two years before flooding."

They live in the middle of that fire area that's going on in northern Saskatchewan now. They're about 90 miles from the La Ronge that all the talking is about. She sent me a picture of where they put a fire break up and it's probably three or four blocks from her house. So they're on their way home. They evacuated and they left early they had to leave the dogs behind. They have someone sitting the house and sitting the dogs. He promised that if he couldn't get them out in evacuation, he'd take them to the lake and let them go in the water, but so far—I think it's starting to rain up there and cool down a little bit so they're hoping they can get back in. But my daughter has no idea what they're going back to as far as smoke damage or anything else.

Tina: No, smoke and flood damage is...

Barbara: And my granddaughter is going to summer school 'cause she didn't pass her math so she is in Prince Albert going to summer school. Didn't she get $84 for being an evacuee.

Tom: You get *paid* when you evacuate?

Barbara: Apparently out there they did anyway 'cause everyone who got evacuated was housed in hotels and it was just to make life a little easier—buy the essentials for life: shampoo, toothpaste, because they left everything to get out.

Tina: You took your body and went.

Barbara: It was a forced evacuation. A few stayed that refused to go and they are looking after the little community they are in—about a thousand in the community plus our two dogs. One of the dogs was mine—it's her dog now but it was mine so I'm getting a little concerned they're both big dogs.

Summer

Lightning

Tina: This is about a time when I was 14. I was born and raised in Manitoba so this in my hometown in Silverfelt(?), Manitoba. We were caretakers of the church which was a humongous large church.

Tom: What flavour was it?

Tina: Protestant. I've been a Catholic for so long I don't remember. My baby brother's and I were in the dining room. The boys were sitting with their backs to the big window and they were working at the table, and I was standing watching them from the opposite side. My mother was sewing in the bedroom—she was making some clothes for the boys. My sister—I don't remember where she was. I was the oldest. It was storming, raining—a stormy day—that's why the kids were all inside. It got stormier and darker. Dad was away at work. It was a dirt road we lived on. The next thing I knew it was lightning and thunder, fairly heavy, but I didn't think anything of it. A little while later... this part of the story I do not remember—my baby brother told me and my mother told me... Nick kept calling me 'cause he was sitting there, wanting some help with his pictures that he was colouring. I'm told I wasn't listening to him—just facing the window with hands on the table looking outside—frozen by the lightning that hit the church. I didn't know this until later on. Nick went crying to my mother; there was something wrong with me. So mother came over and she said it took her 15 minutes to bring me back from unconsciousness or whatever it was that had happened to me.

I'm told I looked at her and said, "What's wrong?"

She had been crying and the babies had both been crying. We didn't think much of it. I was fine—she checked me, not hurt or anything, and we didn't realize what had happened until—when it was bad weather we went to the road to see if Dad had gotten stuck or if he was on his way home—we went to the gate. We had to go past the back end of the church and when we got there we saw bricks lying on the ground. I couldn't figure out what they were doing there. When I looked up, the chimney wasn't there—it was down on the ground. You could also see the rusted heads of each nail on the side of the church—they had all been turned rusty. We went past. There was only one window on that side; the shutters were closed so we didn't pay attention to the windows. But when we got to the road—and I was still wondering about these bricks on the ground—I turned around and saw that one of the shutters from the roadside had opened and the windows were all smashed. What has happened? We didn't really know until we saw Dad coming down and he was able to make the road.

When he got into the yard he said, "What's wrong?"

I said, "Look at the chimney of the church. It's down here—not up there."

Then he looked around and every window in that building was shattered— 4 windows on each side one on the end and two windows on the entrance side. There was not a glass that wasn't broken. [Background] Wow!

He said it had to be lightning. He said that's the only explanation that there is. All the nails were rusty you couldn't see them other that—they had been painted. So that was the only explanation that there is. And the mess inside—unreal.

Lightning rods

Richard: Thunderstorms back when we were kids—it would rock the roof of the house.

Tina: Oh yes.

Richard: And the rain and the lightning would be forking to the ground, but in the last 10 or 15 years, there hasn't been anything.

Barbara: Hardly anything.

Tina: I'm still waiting for a [real] thunderstorm here and I still haven't found one yet. They're not like what we had out in Manitoba or Ontario.

Barbara: Yeah, and that old forked lightning come right down to the ground.

Richard: Been about 20 years since we had a storm—lightning—because I know a fellow that tries to sell lightning rods. He's not having much luck. It's the last thing they'll buy.

Barbara: Well I've got lightning rods on my house, 'cause ours was struck twice already and I figured twice, okay. Three times I'm not wanting to be here.

Tina: [describing a lightning strike] We had a lightning rod—our driveway and the fence for the cattle was on that side—it hit the post on this side—the house was over here. It went underneath the ground. The lightning rod was on the corner. It bypassed the lightning rod, went in the house, and took away my TV set. We came home and we wondered, why did the house look so grey on this one corner? Went inside—my daughter, she was just a little thing— she went to turn on the TV and she said, "Mom the TV's broken. You come and fix it."

I went over and looked at it. "I'm so sorry dear, I can't fix it. I have to get you a new one."

Barbara: The first time it hit our house—our house is on a grade coming up from the water. It's basically to the almost to the top of the hill and so it attracted a lot of—it was higher ground. The first time it hit, my Dad was sitting by the table, and it came in the telephone and traveled all along the window around the corner and blew out to plugs over by the kitchen sink. So that was okay they survived that and got over the shock, and about two years later it came in again, and it didn't come in the telephone this time, it came in—I don't know if it was a window or where—but anyway we had a Keymac stove—you know the old Keymac stove—it threw all the covers off the stove— they went flying. So at that point Dad got on the telephone and called a man out in Pownal that used to install lightning rods.

Richard: Ron Smith.

Barbara: So we're grounded. We've got several lightning hot rods on the house and the grounds running down. You could always see the weather coming and when it came it came right directly in our window.

Richard: I done the barns. Now the new owner—the grounds are all broke.

Barbara: Is that right? Well it was a good thing to have it on the barns because that's where all the hay was stored. A spark would set off a fire pretty easy.

Richard: If the house got struck you could get out, but if the barns got struck...

Richard: Everybody was saying, "Why don't you do the house?"

Tina: We had two—one at each end of the barn

Richard: But the new owner, he's not looking. The grounds are all...

Barbara: Is that right? Aw, what a sin. It used to be a matter of pride to keep your farm up: the barns nicely painted and the rooms done.

Richard: This fella was from Ontario that done it.

Whitewash

Barbara: And we always had to have our fences painted—well we'd whitewash them. The old saying, "Can't afford paint and too proud to whitewash," but we always used to whitewash the fences and then when it would rain it would be the awfulest looking thing and as soon as the sun came out and dried them they'd just be sparkling white, 'cause we whitewashed them.

Richard: Whitewash was all the [thing] back then.

Barbara: And what an awful job whitewashing was—all those little posts.

Richard: You couldn't hardly buy it now, could you?

Barbara: I don't know if you can. It was some kind of lime wasn't it? But, boy, it would sparkle after the rain when the sun got on them.

Tom: Isn't that what Tom Sawyer was doing? He conned some people into doing it for him.

Barbara: He was lucky. He had neighbours.

Richard: It was awful white when it was done—it lasted a couple of years.

Barbara: Oh, yeah.

Tina: We used to do the inside of the barn as well as the outside.

Pat: I don't really have too many memories

Richard: And a great job on cow stables.

Barbara: Yup, keep them nice and clean looking.

Eye of the hurricane

Tom: You were on Lake Ontario, right on the shore?

Tina: Yes, Lake Ontario ran down here and we're living up here—I'd say it would be like a five-story building....

Tom: So, fifty, sixty feet—so you were on the edge of a very high cliff with the lake down below.

Tina: I would say there were about 15 feet between the house and where the drop was down for the lake.

Tom: And the hurricane came daytime? Night time?

Tina: Oh, this was before lunch actually. This isn't the beginning of the story—this is kind of in the middle.

Tom: Let's start in the middle and do the ends later. Who was with you?

Tina: My first husband and I were living in cottage #1 which had been renovated. We had another couple that were living in #3. It was just like a summer cottage—there was no renovation there or nothing. We each had a car and when we heard the noise, somebody looked out the window said, "Oh isn't that pretty."

I looked out the window. I said, "No that is not pretty. Let's get those cottages—tear one apart and use the wood to close the windows. That's hurricane!"

[husband]: What? That's just wind.

I said, "If you don't believe me you go sit outside. I'm staying in here I'm going to close everything, and if you're not coming in—I don't want you to stay outside because I don't want you to go away with the hurricane." We tore the cottage that they were living—we tore that one apart, used the lumber from that one to cover the windows, to cover the doors, because the noise we heard. And I mean your nerves—you're really hyper in that because you see it coming and you see all that other stuff that's coming ahead of it and you know it's not just the wind.

Tom: Was the wind coming from offshore?

Tina: It was coming from Lake Ontario

Tom: So there weren't any houses our trucks are things blowing across.

Tina: She came right into Ontario from the city onto the lake, right across the lake, picking up farm buildings and cattle and stuff. She's coming down our way.

Tom: But those [things picked up by the wind] presumably dropped into the water before they got to you? Were there things blowing?

Tina: Oh yes. If the weather doesn't slow down—if they were not in the middle. If they ended up in the middle [the eye] they'd fall, but if they never got to the middle—if they stayed on the outside, which is the hurricane itself, then they would stay in there. After the storm we found parts of boats and parts of animals and stuff like that parts of animals and you could see...

Tom: Parts of animals?

Tina: Yes. That's what I mean it isn't something that's easy. It is very difficult to describe. While we were trying to get those windows covered and nailed down so they wouldn't get open, we could see this, and we had to rush. We had two cars there yet in front of our Cottage was at a tree, a space, a tree here, a space, and another tree. And the two cars in-between—that's what the boys were doing. I was getting his wife to hold the lumber for me so I could nail it 'cause I knew what I was doing—I'm a carpenter. I was nailing it while she was holding it. the boys brought the cars in. They had found chains that were in the last Cottage. They were chaining the two cars to the two trees and then to the centre tree. So we figured that would hold them. While they were doing that, she and I were doing the windows and when we got to the door—now I'm fine—I could do it here—at that time you were kind of shaky because you were watching in and you were are hearing the noise from the hurricane itself and the wind and all that—it's got your adrenaline going full speed ahead. I mean, mentally I don't know what was going on in my brain, but all it was doing was telling me to get that done see if I could help to save the four of us.

Tom: And you were saved.

Tina: Yes, we were.

Tom: The cottage stood?

Tina: When the hurricane got to the cottage there, all of a sudden everything went quiet.

Tom: So the eye went right over?

Tina: Yes. My husband, he went over and he started taking a sheet of plywood that I had in front of the door—he started taking it off. I happened to have been in the other room, and I came in and I looked at him and said, What are you doing?

He said, "I'm taking it off. The hurricane is over."

"No it's not over. You're in the middle of the eye."

Tom: It's going to go the other way next.

Tina: "The other end is coming over. After the eye goes the rest of it's coming over and you got all that stuff that's left hanging in there from the hurricane itself. That's going to come pounding on the building." He didn't believe me.

I said, "If you want to go outside, go outside. But I'm lockin' the door right behind you. And I'm nailing that wall back shut."

He looked at me.

Tom: So you say this was your first husband. Did you lose him?

Tina: I'd only been married to him for two months. So I told Buck and his wife, "You grab a hold of him—hold him there. I can handle this."

He had only pulled part of it off. They took him and held him down while I finished nailing it up. When I got finished nailing, here comes the other half [of the hurricane].

He looked at me and he said, "How did you know that?"

I said, "It's a hurricane. We're in the eye of the hurricane. The other part's got to come over yet. The second half is worse than the first half.

Barbara: You're on the back side of it.

Tina: It's got all kinds of stuff going through. You don't know what's in there, what's going to hit your building. I described it, but it's still not the same as seeing it.

Tom: A lot of noise?

Tina: So yes, fantastic! I described it to somebody one day, it sounds like two trains running through your building all at the same time—like the two engines.

Barbara: In Cottages it would be worse than in the homes because they're a little more frail.

Tina: And not only that, we were out in the open. There was nothing around there. They had bought the property and they had built the cottages there and there was absolutely— except for those three trees—there was nothing to save us.

Barbara: It hit here at night. Pretty wild. We were at a neighbour's place—my Mom and Dad and when we had to go home—I don't need to record this.

Tom: Sure you do.

Tina: You might as well add on to it.

Barbara: When we went to go home, we had an old 53 Chev' truck, a bit of a grinder, and we were in that. We left our neighbours and we were sliding around pretty well 'cause there was a heavy, heavy rain with it as well. We get down the road as far as our land and we couldn't get up the lane. The water was coming down and the mud was so deep we had to turn around and go back through this hurricane, and go all the way around it was about 2 miles—maybe 3—and come in what we called our back lane—the cattle

Seasons and weather: Summer

lane for driving the horses and cows back to the pasture. That was more grassy. It would grow when there was no traffic on it, so we got enough traction—it was about a half mile long too. We could get enough traction just barely to make it home and into the house. The winds were so high! It was one of the most devastating hurricanes that we had in Canada to that time.

Tina: It was the most expensive hurricane that's ever been in Canada. In this report that I'm looking for it'll give you the exact amount. There's never been another hurricane that cost that much or spent that much time in Canada, going from one end to the other end. Where we were there at the cottage there was—about two miles away—is where they had a canal for the boats to go through it was on the Queen Elizabeth Highway. It was a bridge that lifted up when the boat went through then went back down.

Barbara: Drawbridge.

Tina: It was loaded with cars I don't know how many cars were on there, how many cars went in the water because of the hurricane going through.

Barbara: It was enough.

Tina: In the morning my husband and I had planned to visit my family (this should be at the beginning) because we had just been married and we were going to go visit them. I was going to introduce them to him. But in the morning when I woke up, I was so sick I couldn't even get out of bed and there was nothing wrong with me when I went to sleep, but that was what was telling me, don't go. If we woulda gone what would have been on the middle on that bridge when it went. That's part of... if you want excitement don't ask for a hurricane.

Barbara: Where were you in Hurricane Hazel, Richard?

Richard: What year was that?

Barbara: '54

Tom: You were born then?

[general laughter]

Barbara: He must be a lot of younger than I am.

Richard: I don't remember, was Hazel the worst one we had?

Tina: She's the worst one Canada has ever had.

Richard: My nephew and I were out spreading manure and we were going down through my uncle's yard and I seen it coming across the fields and the woods, so we had no choice but to go into the barn so we took a chance on going into the barn—we didn't know whether it was a good choice—the barn was rocking. That's the highlight—after that we waited until it calmed down. It took a roof off the barn at Leo McIsaac's coming across—it came right across from Stratford, right across and then kept on going. It didn't last that long—about an hour.

Barbara: Ours lasted quite a long time it was about...

Richard: It was headed toward your place.

Barbara: It was headed right toward Alice Ross's living room.

Tina: I know we had quite a time of it.

Barbara: The next morning the boys' tent was just little shards hanging from the trees in the apple orchard. They arrived in about 9:30. They were soaked, and scared.

Richard: There wasn't a big amount of destruction here on the Island.

Tom: It must have been tapering off by then.

Barbara: I think it might have been blowing out.

Tina: Down our way we got the main of it. It went right over our building.

Barbara: You weren't in Ontario the time the tornado went through were you?

Tina: Hurricane Hazel?

Barbara: No No. This would be a tornado. This would be in 1970 something.

Tina: No I was living in Ontario then.

Barbara: You were living in Ontario?

Tina: Yeah, in Edwards, Ontario.

Barbara: That's what I'm saying, were you living there when the tornado went through?

Tina: Yeah, but we didn't get very much, we just got a lot of wind.

Barbara: Well I was in Toronto that summer when it went through and I remember waking up and there was just absolute silence in Toronto and you know that's pretty unreal in Toronto. I don't think anything ever stopped up there, but it was just dead silence. It went from Toronto north through the area where they grow all the really good stuff—between there and Barrie, Ontario. It went right through there—terrible crop devastation. I don't think there was any loss of life but the crops were all devastated and they were saying about the onion fields that the onions...

Tina: Yeah, I remember that.

Barbara: They were so deep in onions, it was so slick, you couldn't walk through the onion field. We have had a few Moments in Canada.

Tina: But she was not as bad as Hazel was.

ACTIVITIES

Church/Sundays

I heard every word you sang

Neil: In his early years my father's parents were strong in the Baptist tradition. As he got older, he sort of strayed from the church. When he was in later years, he started going again. He joined the church and became an elder. At the age of 67 he wanted to be baptized in the Baptist tradition, by submersion [immersion] in water.

There is another incident stays with me. When we knew that my sister was going to be married, his health was not too good. We weren't sure if he was going to be there, but he was. I sang at my sister's wedding. When the service was over, he came to me and said, "I am hard of hearing but I heard every word you sang." He usually did *not* give out compliments. Carl Brydon died on October 3, 1966, on his 43rd wedding anniversary. His younger brother died the exact same day, thirteen years later.

Our church

Donna: As a child of the 40's and 50's in rural PEI. the church was an extremely important part of my growth. The church was the centre of our family's social life. The fact that we had no vehicle, and that the church was only a five minute walk away, meant we spent a lot of time at the church.

I remember Sunday School as being another hour in a classroom. We were expected to know our assigned memory work, sometimes as many as six to eight verses! Preparation for this could not be left until Saturday afternoon. Friday night Young People's meetings were less work and a lot more fun. Corn boils, wiener roasts, skating parties and sing-songs hold fond memories.

Activities: Church/Sundays

Daddy was the church's grave digger, fire starter, furnace stoker, bell ringer, grass cutter, custodian, (and an elder) all for very meagre monetary rewards. Mom was always a member of the choir and often the organist.

Beginning at an early age, Saturday afternoons were a time for myself and my sisters to dust the church pews while Mom swept the sanctuary. I remember how pleased we were when we found the occasional penny, nickel or dime. Daddy would give us permission to keep the treasures, but Mom would use it as a teaching Moment and we were usually left feeling guilty. My sister remembers other treasures such as the gum on the bottom of the pews, but I chose to remember Daddy's permission as the best part of the cleaning ritual.

I will always remember the stress of my Mom on the Saturday prior to Communion Sunday. One of her duties was to wash and iron the linen table cloths. This was not easy with flat irons and a wood stove. My sisters and I would help in these special preparations by shining the silver communion service.

As teenagers, my sisters and I were always excited if there was a Saturday wedding performed in the church. We would sneak into the balcony and pass judgements on the brides' dresses and the choice of colours for the bridesmaids.

One of the biggest events of the year was the tea party held in the hardwood grove outside the church. This was the place where the horses were tied during service. In those days most everyone traveled by horse and wagon. But on Saturday each summer this area was transformed into a country kitchen. This was more than a tea party. This was a full course chicken dinner! Today the Department of Health would be horrified, but it was the highlight of the summer when I was a child. I cannot recall any episodes of food poisoning!

Summer was always the time for the return of family and friends from places such as Boston or Toronto. I can remember Mom, suddenly realizing in the middle of the sermon, that there was someone in the congregation who should be invited for lunch. Quickly she made a list of things needed and my sister was sent running down the hill to McPherson's store. The store, of course, was not open on Sunday, but Dan and Katherine would never see us in a fix.

I remember, too, the laughs we children had one Sunday when we realized

Mom had appeared at service with her apron over her Sunday dress.

I recall, also, a Sunday when I spent the entire hour spelling the word printed on the top of the song book. I kept repeating the letters H—Y—M—N—S until I was home and able to ask Mom "What is this word?"

I remember the Sunday service I sat with a very painful foot. I had stepped on a nail the previous day and it was fine when I left for Sunday School, but with each passing moment my foot was getting bigger and bigger and sorer and sorer. I can't recall if I visited the doctor, but probably a soak with water and Epsom salts was all that was needed. Antibiotics were not given as freely in those days.

The church was a playground for me and my siblings—hide and seek among the headstones, while our father worked at one of the many tasks.

There was so much fun; running home following Young People's or Evening Service; laughing and squealing with the thought that if we slowed down the many bats in the evening sky would get in our hair. Belfries are a favourite home for bats.

Our church was more than the place of learning, worshipping and socializing. It was part of our heritage. A beautiful structure, built by our forefathers in the year 1823, historical St. John's Presbyterian Church continues to be an integral part of this PEI community.

Dad and Ministers

Arlene: Mom was active with the church. Dad didn't go to church but he knew every minister in town. I remember looking out, and he'd be standing on a street corner surrounded by ministers. What they were talking about, I don't know.

[We all laughed, picturing it in our minds.]

Mary: Solving the mysteries of life.

Arlene: Yes. And when he died the whole town closed down. Every store closed down. He was a very quiet man. Mom was the talker. He was very active, he was a fireman and in the Legion."

Getting ready

Dora: Saturday night we had our once-a-week bath. We had to polish the shoes and have everything laid out Saturday night for Sunday morning. We walked to the Baptist church in the morning for service, and then we'd walk home. Then we had to go to church Sunday afternoon, which we didn't appreciate very much. If there was church, we had to be there.

Walking to church

Dora: There was only one woman in the community with a car and she wouldn't stop and pick anybody up in the car. She'd just go to church and park her car. She had somebody else drive it because she couldn't drive it. I guess one of her family broke the car. It was a big joke to us; we were walking along 'cause she wouldn't pick us up, eh?

[And we all laughed and shook our heads—we all knew people like that.]

Sunday afternoons

Dora: On Sunday, during the summer afternoons, our family always came home and we'd have a picnic. We had two big cherry trees in our yard, and my father built a big picnic table that went from one tree to the other. So the older ones always had a place to sit, and the rest of the kids all sat on the lawn when we had our picnic.

Catholicism and Fundamentalism

Richard: My idea of religion wouldn't probably go along with everybody else. I figure one is enough.

Tom: But you said your background was Catholic.

Richard: My situation—I'm Catholic—I've seen so many changes that they made to make it easier;

Tom: You said it was hard in the old days.

Richard: In the old days it was cruel, some of the things they expected you to do. For example, if you wanted to go to Holy Communion you had to fast from midnight, and the majority of the congregation was farmers. They had to get up and they had to do all their farm chores in the morning and then go to service, and they wouldn't get a bite till dinner-time, which is unheard of now. Another example is Lent. Now Lent today, they don't close off dances or card parties like they did back in the old days.

Tom: They shut those down?

Richard: When I was young, Lent was something that I didn't look forward to. You had to give up something—a lot of alcoholics gave up drinking.

Tom: Did they really do it?

Richard: Yeah. Soon as it was over Easter…the Saturday before Easter…. They shut down all the entertainment.

Tom: At least the Catholics did.

Richard: I don't know about the other services. But there was a lot of traditions that are not around today, and you'd wonder why you had to do them. Confession is one. Now there's hardly anybody goes to confession.

Tom: So what was it like, going to confession?

Richard: Oh, it was cruel for me because I had a speech problem. I'd be shaking like a leaf, so I figure I should get there after going through all that.

Tom: Oh, to Heaven, you mean. So, were you told to do things?

Richard: Oh yeah.

Tom: What did you have to do?

Richard: You had to bare your soul and you had to tell how long it was since you were at confession. Then if you were honest and told everything you done wrong, he'd tell you to mend your ways, so to speak. It has gone out of date. There's hardly anyone goes now.

Tom: Is that right. So where did you live when you were going?

Richard: This was in Vernon River, St. Joachim's. I used to be an altar boy. There was altar boys back then—there still is.

Tom: So what did an altar boy do?

Richard: There was two stages of altar boys back then—there was the senior group and a junior group. The ones with more experience had more to do with the mass.

Another big change—the mass was in Latin back in my early days and then they done away with Latin.

And then the altar was a big altar at the back and the priest faced the altar instead of facing the people, so they done away with the altar—well, it's still there but they don't use it. Now they just have just a table out front and they face the people.

So the changes were unreal in the Catholic religion. I'm not versed on the other religions whether there were that many changes or not. You wonder if the old people are going to be—how shall I put it—rewarded [in Heaven] for all those sacrifices they had to make.

[Ethel]: Have a muffin.

Richard: If I'd a known this, I wouldn't have gone to McDonald's!

Tom: I grew up in a Protestant Church. It was closer to what you call Fundamentalist, and I wrote a book about looking at some of what's in [the Bible]—they claim whatever the Bible said that's what they believe. Well, take drinking. The group I was in said that drinking alcoholic beverages was—the Bible was against it. I just assumed it was, and somewhere in my early twenties we were invited to dinner by some people across the way in our apartment and they offered us wine with dinner.

"Oh, I don't drink. I'm a Christian."

"Oh, that's interesting, we're Christians too. Why do you believe that?"

"Oh it's in the Bible. I'll go find it and show you."

And so I went looking, and I discovered there was nothing about [alcoholic] abstinence—abstain from fleshly lusts

Richard: Wine was always part of our service.

Tom: Oh yeah. Well it wasn't part of the Fundamentalist service! Grape juice. In fact I've heard people who claimed that Jesus turned the water into grape juice, not into wine. But when I went to look, I discovered there was nothing about abstinence. Temperance just said be moderate in all things you do—it wasn't talking about alcohol. I *finally* discovered that the Bible did have some things to say about drunkenness, and the preachers I'd heard had taken these passages about drunkenness and transferred over into any drinking at all, which of course is not—of course it's bad to get drunk, no arguing about that, but they had translated that differently.

Richard: Another tradition that's gone, they used to have what they called a mission. It would last for a week and they'd get those speakers. Oh, they'd be from all over, American, whatever, and they'd preach fire and brimstone, for a whole week.

Tom: Catholic?

Richard: Scare you.

Tom: Catholic preachers! I didn't know Catholics were into fire and brimstone.

Richard: That's the way I describe it. You'd wonder how you were supposed to increase the population if you listened to them folks—you weren't supposed to touch anyone of the opposite gender. Such a bunch of nonsense you never heard in your life.

Tom: Even when you got married?

Richard: We weren't supposed to even look at anybody until you get married, hardly—well you could look at them, but that would be it. What a bunch of nonsense. And then with pedophiles among their congregation. So that's all gone. Thank God, that's gone.

Tom: The pedophiles are gone?

Richard: No the old missions. Pedophiles are not gone, no.

Tom: So do you remember any scandals in your church?

Richard: Not in our area, but there's all kinds of scandals.

Tom: Well, there are a lot more scandals recently.

Richard: Just coming out now. The last 25 or 30 years they're uncovering them. It's not only Catholics, you know.

Prayer to St. Therese

Helen: A lady in Boston introduced me to the prayer to St. Therese—she was saying the prayer for her daughter who had left for Ontario and was seeking work there when, at that moment, her son came into the house with a rose which he gave to her. A couple of days later her daughter called to report that she had obtained a job.

Well, I was sceptical of this story, to say the least, until one day I needed a 'big favour'. I started saying the prayer and to my dismay I received *many* roses and my favour was granted. Roses from this beautiful Saint's heavenly

Activities: Church/Sundays

garden!

[Ed: the extensive background information about St. Therese has been omitted to keep the focus on Helen's personal experience. I'm sure she will be happy to share more details if you ask.]

Hillcrest Gospel Singers Songbook]

There is Power in the Blood	Sweet Hour of Prayer
The Grumbler's Song	I Love To Tell The Story
The Old Country Church	In The Shade of the Family Tree
When the Roll is Called Up Yonder	Brethren We Have Met To Worship
What a Friend We Have in Jesus	Keep On the Sunny Side
Life is Like a Mountain Railroad	The Old Rugged Cross
This World is Not My Home	Near The Cross
The Lily of the Valley	Church in The Wildwood
Love Lifted Me	I'll Fly Away
There's A Land that is Fairer than Day	I'm Going To Live So God Can Use Me
Give Me Oil For My Lamp	How Beautiful Heaven Must Be
Stand Up, Stand Up For Jesus	The Garden
I am Thine O Lord	Higher Ground
Jesus Hold My Hand	Turn Your Radio On
Farther Along	Angel Band (My Latest Son)
Amazing Grace	My Saviour's Love
Where The Roses Never Fade	Lord I'm Coming Home
This World Is Not My Home	I Heard My Saviour Calling Me
Leaning On The Everlasting Arms	Since Jesus Came Into My Heart

Lead Me To Calvary	The Gloryland Way
My Saviour First of All	Just Over In the Gloryland
The Unclouded Day	I Saw the Light

Going to Town

Dances in Montague

dd: I remember when Don Messer would play for the dances in the Beaver Club in Montague. I lived in Abney. We would walk to get the bus in Murray River and go to the dances. On the return trip we would still have the long walk home from the bus. And we still had to get up the next morning to go to Sunday School.

One night after getting off the bus on Saturday night after the dance, two of my cousins, Rita and Audrey Bell, and I were walking down the railroad track. It came up a snow storm, so we got into the station building, stoked up the fire and stayed through the night.

Dances all the time

Tina: Myrtle was saying something about dancing.

Peggy: Oh yes, I went to dances when I was old enough—went to dances all the time—used to be dances in our own school, right handy, and we used to go there all the time. When I was teaching in Glen Cove we'd go to dances. We'd go standing on the back of the truck—that's the way you went. There'd be crowds on them.

Tina: What type of music did they have then?

Peggy: Oh, good fiddle music. Oh yes, some of those old fiddlers, Buddy MacMaster he was around and started off playing at the dances a little older than me—not much—and then when I got older when I left home, there was dances and cèilidhs all the time. I would go to a dance when I was in Halifax, the Cape Breton Club—the PEI Club had a dance on Thursday night, and the [Barn Tent?] Club on Friday night, the Cape Breton Club had a dance on Saturday night. That was the people that worked there and they went to them—all the dances and to go to shows then too. Every night was full. Every party there was I went to them, that's what I wanted, until we got married—well, then it was different. I was home with the kids—that was okay. They all grew up, and then I went again! Dances and cèilidhs and parties. You know it's just kind of the way my life went.

Activities

Miriam: We always went to church morning and evening. We walked to Eldon to the movies and later years to the dances

BIRTHDAYS

Premier birthday party

Tom: Pat, okay tell us about a birthday party you remember.

Pat: The birthday I remember most was when I was 10 years old. I was evacuated from England when I was 9 ½ and spent a few months on PEI getting adjusted, living with these wonderful people, and when my tenth birthday came they decided I could invite anybody I wanted so I invited just about all the class, because I had just started school and had all these new friends. Of course being somewhat of a celebrity, the newspapers picked it up, and the radio.

Tom: Because you were an evacuee?

Pat: Yeah. I was a September baby and it was a beautiful September day, and all these classmates turned up and walked and cars and stuff. There was this big limousine came up the driveway. Out came the Premier of PEI who was named Thane Campbell—you probably remember. This sort of threw my foster mother, because she wasn't prepared to entertain celebrities—just kids. Anyway, rising to the tasks she offered him a cup of tea and he stayed and glad-handed everybody—all us little kids—we were potential voters when we grew up. After he done all this, I had to have my picture taken with him. That was really big—that made the paper the next day.

When the article reached our house, my foster mother said, "Now you cut out the picture and you send it to your mother in England and tell her what happened."

So I was forced to sit down and write a letter and no kids likes to write letters. Anyway I went into great detail about my birthday party, and of course when she got the letter, she was all excited—the Premier had come to her daughter's birthday, but they didn't called it Premier it was Prime Minister so it came out in our neighbourhood of Wembley where we had lived that the prime minister of Canada had come to my birthday it and she still has the clipping to this day. The cake was amazing. She used to make this boiled icing and she made a great big cake—two layer cake—because I think there was probably about 20 kids, and it was just huge and it was an amazing cake and an amazing day and that was me being 10.

Barbara: You being 10 sounds very good.

Toughest cake

Pat: This isn't really very exciting. When my five children were growing up when it came time for their birthday, they all got to pick what kind of cake they want, and everybody had something different so that was fine—it was their day—but my son who still lives down in lower Montague, his was favourite was the Jell-O cake. Now anybody who said Jell-O cake knows how to make it. You make the angel food cake and then you poke holes in it and you pour hot Jell-O and then when it's upended you've got this beautiful

Activities: Birthdays 51

rainbow cake. And he still wants me to make his Jell-O cake and he's 62, for heaven's sake.

Tom: Do you make it?

Pat: No I gave up baking years ago—been there, did that.

Barbara: Speaking of angel food cakes, my kids were like that too—they got their choice of cake, and the cakes get higher and more elaborate as the years went on until finally it got to the point—one of my daughter's birthdays always happened to be a kind of a muggy day, and you can't make good cake and you certainly can't make boiled icing on a muggy day. So one year I decided I was going to make an angel food cake 'cause no matter what you do an angel food cake comes out nice and high, and I made it, and it had sprinkles on the inside and I cut it in half and made the boiled icing and frosted it and then I had coloured Smarties all around it a Happy Birthday Jenny on it with lots of candles. They were all excited. They'd played games and they'd made more mess than you could shake a stick at, and they'd opened gifts and gotten all chocolaty and everything, and they had hot dogs and Kool-Aid and then the cake game. We all sang Happy Birthday, blew out the candles, and then I started cutting the cake. An angel food cake is traditional not that soft. I have to have a knife in hot water to cut it. This one little boy was sawing at his piece of cake and he's had a spoon instead of a fork.

So that was a disadvantage but he kept digging at this cake, "This cake is

tough boy oh boy this cake is tough. This cake is the toughest cake I've ever had."

So it was my one lesson—don't give young kids angel food cake ever again. And now my daughter makes cakes—she makes trains, she makes those telephone booths—Doctor Who, and she uses marzipan, and she makes dragon cakes and I'm thinkin', if I hadn't of had boiled icing, I wouldn't have had cake. That was my only hope for a nice cake.

Topped with 50 candles

Pat: My friend in New Brunswick had taken a course in cake making and cake decorating and she wanted to try it out. She had just graduated and she said to me, "Do you mind if I make your birthday cake for you?"

And I said, "Wonderful."

And so she said, "Now what would you like, chocolate or white?"

I said, "Well, you surprise me."

She had all these fancy tins. I was 50 years old and I thought this was a special birthday and here this friend was going to make a special cake for me.

So she phoned me just before supper-time and said, "Will you come down and pick up the cake? I don't have transportation."

So I loaded my littlest one in the back of the car and I drove down to her place. If she thought she was going to surprise me, she certainly did, because this cake was beautifully scalloped and decorated, but it had 50 candles on it—green candles. You could hardly see the top of the cake. I guess I had a surprised look on my face. I thanked her profusely, loaded my littlest one and the cake into the back of the car.

I got home and I looked at him and I said, "What are we gonna do with this cake?"

He got his little stool and he dragged it to the counter, and he stood on his stool and we removed all the candles, and we got a knife and we smoothed the top of the cake. He had a wonderful time licking and making a mess.

So when I said, "Well how many candles we gonna put back on?" so it was tradition in our house that you added the first number to the second number, so 50 only amounted to five candles. So we put the five candles back, and it looks as if somebody had ploughed the top of the cake. My older son came home and as a special occasion, he brought me a bottle of saki. I'd never had saki and he thought that would be a surprise—oh second surprise of the day. That was lovely. We didn't start on that until after supper, and meanwhile my sister-in-law who I love dearly and always brought something exotic for my birthday, she brought me a kimono—a beautiful red kimono with swirls all over it. So it turned out the Japanese party. We ate cake, we drank Sake and I pranced around in this wonderful kimono. There you go, 50 years to remember.

Flamingos on the lawn

Tom: You didn't get flamingos in your lawn? I'd never heard of that until....

Pat: That was recent—not going back 50 years, was it?

Tom: The flamingos in the lawn?

Barbara: Oh maybe thirty years. I can remember in Charlottetown in the eighties. Getting flamingos on the lawn then.

Pat: They used to wait until you went to bed and then they'd put flamingos on your lawn. Surprise!

Tom: I had never heard of this, having lived in the states, until I saw it on the cover one of the For Better For Worse collections,. It shows her husband looking out. It was totally lost on me, what on earth it was doing.

Barbara: Especially since there's not a pink flamingo within 1000 miles of Canada.

Pat: I don't know how it originated.

Tom: It seems pretty silly.

Pat: When I was living in British Columbia the neighbour woke up to a whole lawn full.

Tom: My wife threatens me on my 60th birthday that she was going to rent a yard full of flamingos.

I said, "Well.... I hope not."

She made up a drawing with flamingos instead put 60 of them in the drawing. I don't know if you'd call it embarrassing. How would you feel?

Tina: I would die laughing.

Pat: Being an exhibitionist, I would just love it.

Tina: They threaten me with it. I laughed so hard I guess they changed their mind.

Tom: They decided it would be a waste of money.

Richard: This is a stupid question. What are they?

Barbara: They're like a stork that stands on one leg and they are a bright coral pink.

Richard: Are they alive?

Barbara: No, no, they're just plastic on stands.

Tina: There are live ones. They have some in Niagara Falls.

Barbara: In Florida they have a lot of them.

Tom: Yeah there's lots of them down in the south.

Richard: The size of a swan?

Barbara: They're a crane.

Tom: Think of a heron, a little bigger than a heron and probably just as annoying I imagine.

Tina: They can make quite a bit of noise.

Barbara: The only time I ever saw them was at Victoria and they had some in the butterfly garden there. One area was just for flamingos in Victoria.

First birthday cakes

Tom: Anybody remember first birthdays of your children? Seems to me I remember our son, he sat in his high chair—first, second, I'm not sure—and it was a chocolate cupcake and it was just like total chocolate, face, tray, everywhere.

Barbara: The thing nowadays is to give it to them and let them go for it.

Tina: Take his clothes off from the waist up. My grandson went through it. He was chocolate up to his waist.

Tom: And happy as a clam.

Tina: Oh yes, was he happy.

Barbara: I have a picture at home of my first birthday and my Dad had made me—I don't think there was such a thing as high chairs in those days—well there were but we didn't have one. He had a chair that he had made and it had a tray that went across. So I'm there in all my glory with my short hair all cut in the bowl cut [put a bowl over the head and cut off all the hair below it] and I had this dress that was smocked to the nth degree and it looks white in that picture—black and white—and I'm out on the front lawn and in my special chair with my tray and there's a big cake there with one candle on it. That's all I have; I don't have a memory of ever eating the cake—I suppose I did—but I often look at it and wonder, how did they ever clean that dress 'cause I'm sure it was a gorgeous dress and I'm there just ready to pounce on this one candle that's burning.

Pat: They used to do some amazing smocking didn't they. I never mastered it but my little girls always had smocked dresses because my beloved sister-in-law used to smock.

Barbara: I have baby dresses at home and I have an old, old doll that was given to my sister. She was born in 1936 and it was an old, old doll then. She's sort of life-size for babies and so I have a lot of baby clothes left that Mom let me keep for this doll. All the smocking across here and the needlepoint work on different ones. They were beautiful, beautiful dresses. I have one that's a cap—a bonnet—and it's lined inside with orange and it's kind of a charcoal outside, and then the cape lined with orange and charcoal—she must have been pretty fancy when she was in that.

LIBRARIES & READING

The joy of our local library

Donna: My childhood was spent in rural PEI but out family felt privileged to have a public library just a few miles from home. It was a place of enjoyment and adventure for us all.

Saturday afternoon was our time to choose our reading for the week. My sister, Carolyn, and I would rush around in the morning completing our assigned chores: dry mopping the bedrooms, dusting the parlour furniture, and scrubbing and waxing the kitchen and pantry floors. This was done on hands and knees, and it was important the task be equally divided. When we met at the seam in the linoleum, we were free to go.

The two mile walk was difficult for young legs but the reward made it worthwhile. The library was an interesting and beautiful room to us. It was located in the front room of one of the finest farm houses in the community—a room of magic! It had mahogany shelves reaching from floor to ceiling. They were usually well-stocked with the popular books of the '50s and '60s. The librarian's desk was nestled in the bay window overlooking the fields. I can still remember the pleasant aroma: old leather, new leather, paper, ink, and in the winter the wonderful smell of wood smoke.

Esther, the librarian, was a kind and pleasant lady, always patient as our young minds struggled to decide which three books would be our choice for the week. She was very knowledgeable about her books and always seemed able to suggest something we would enjoy. Books by Emily Loring, Laura Lee Hope, Zane Grey, the Bronte sisters, C S Lewis, Louis L'Amour, and of course out own Lucy Maude Montgomery were a few of our favourites.

As a young reader I enjoyed books, but was always ready to play 'house' or 'school' or a game of 'leap', 'red rover' or 'mister may I.' My sister, on the other hand, was a constant reader. She always had a book in hand. The wood box by the wood stove was a favoured spot in the winter, and in summer you might find her in the riding sleigh stored in the outbuilding. She was even found enjoying the solitude of the outdoor privy! Daddy was heard many times admonishing her, "Get your nose out of that book and go out to play."

As a senior citizen I can now realize that visiting the library and choosing books is only one of many benefits of being a reader. Reading is adventure, brings knowledge, and allows escape. It transported us to so many interesting places and allowed us to become any one of our favourite characters. Its pleasure does not diminish with age and it even helps with crossword puzzles and cryptograms!

Finally allowed to go

Corena: I remember I read whatever I could lay my hands on 'cause I always loved reading. We couldn't get books from the Montague Library because you had to have them back by a certain time/date and that wasn't easy because sometimes we... well they did have the horse and wagon kind of

Activities: Libraries & Reading

thing and a horse and sleigh but sometimes no vehicle, so I wasn't allowed to get books from the library in Montague. When I moved to Charlottetown that was the big thrill—being able to—when I was old enough...

Tom: How old do you guess you were?

Corena: The first time we moved to Charlottetown, I was just five after I had started school in Lower Montague. Because I had gone for a few months Mom went to Prince Street School and talked to the principal, and he said it would be a shame to hold me back because I had put in so many months, and they let me enter. But when I was in grade four, we came back to Lower Montague and I went to four, five, and six in Lower Montague, and then back to Charlottetown, for good. When I was older I was able to go to the library myself and get books and get them back on time of course or I'd be the one having to pay—from my baby sitting money, probably.

Tom: Do you remember what sort of books you liked?

Corena: *Bobsey Twins*. I remember well—as a matter of fact, I bought it one at a yard sale a few years back. I found a yard sale up in Caledonia where they had some, and I bought some because my friend, Jean was her name, the girl that put the stick in the mailbox [from another early school story], she got these books from relatives, or something, at Christmas, and she would loan them to me. That I treasured.

Tom: Was it The *Bobsey Twins* that had Flossie as the little girl?

Corena: Tom I don't remember.

Tom: It's been a while.

Corena: I have to look. I have a book or two at home of the Bobsey Twins—I just wanted to open them and when I saw them I couldn't resist.

Going by bicycle

Tom: I can remember when I was first, second, third grade we actually lived in the States in a suburb of Chicago, but I had a bicycle, and I was allowed to ride over to the library, which must have been ten fifteen blocks away, by myself. I sometimes wonder how I didn't get run over by a car or something, but I guess things were different in those days, but I can remember discovering these shelves with the children's books and I remember discovering the *Black Stallion* books. They made a movie of one recently but there was a whole series—*The Black Stallion, Son Of The Black Stallion*—it went on and on. I read all of those, and then there were stories about a dog—*Lad Of Sunnybrook Farm* or something and I don't know, anyway, and I would devour them once I latched onto them. Let's see, the guy who could talk to animals—*Dr. Dolittle.* I remember. There's about twenty three books in that series, and I can remember wading through all of those, and just devouring anything that was there. In fact I always used to read leaning on one side, and I think one of my eyes settled in as more nearsighted than the other one from all that time when I was reading with the book with on the bed with my head propped to one side. Anyway the library was a great thing from my viewpoint.

Her nose in a book

Winnie McCormick: My grandmother was a teacher and my uncles and aunts were teachers and there were always books around but there was no library in the country and I wasn't... but I don't know where... of course I had the early books like they read to us— they would always read to us and I couldn't wait...

Tom: Your parents?

Winnie: Probably my grandma and my aunt, because Daddy would be out doing barn work and Mom would be baking biscuits, or bread, or whatever kind of thing, so it was wonderful to have these two teachers. I wanted to read. I went to a one-room SCHOOL and we had from grade one through grade ten. At that time, the teacher put the lessons on the board for the younger kids—you had to copy your math down into your book and then do your work, and the older children would be reading—some of the older grades—and they would stand up at the side of the desk and read just a paragraph or whatever. I couldn't wait till I could finish my work so I could get the rest of the story. *The Ransom of Red Chief, Ichabod Crane and the Headless Horseman,* there were some Bible stories in there too *Peace Be Still* and the one about the oil cruet that never went dry. These books were printed in the States but we used them and you weren't allowed—you didn't buy them, you just used them the year you had them and the next year the one coming behind you had them. Somewhere along the line, I don't know how soon, I found *Anne of Green Gables* and I devoured those. I just loved those. If they couldn't find me they'd ask, "Where is Winifred?"

"Oh she's got her nose in a book."

Corena: That's what my brother used to say about me. He'd get so cross!

Winnie: Then when I was older, I had a neighbour who lived across the way, who used to go to the library and get books, and he would loan them to me because he read them quickly, and one of the favourites was *Zane Grey* and *Perry Mason*—I just love those, and when my aunt was teaching—she taught for awhile further up east—she would go to the library and get books for her school children, and she'd bring them home. She stayed at home for the weekend, so while she was home for the weekend, I would read as much as ever I could get my hands on, and then off she went—she would take them back then. I've been a reader and loved reading all my life.

Tom: Great!

[?]: I found this book that had been left there by a previous person—older, I think—*The Robe* by Lloyd C. Douglas. I couldn't understand it.

Veda: I have a copy of it at home.

[?]: I didn't understand it. It was way beyond—years later I reread it—I didn't understand it, but it was something to read!

Corena: I find a real joy in going to the library. Being surrounded by books that was—that's still a thrill to me—just like the Confederation Centre. It's a thrill to me to go there to productions.

Winnie: I would not be a good employee at the library because I would try to read every book that was in there. [laughter] I wouldn't be doing my work. I would be reading.

OLD HOME WEEK

The Provincial Exhibition

Richard: The Provincial Exhibition is a big attraction.

Tom: OK. Is this in Charlottetown?

Richard: Yeah.

Tom: Kind of like Old Home Week?

Richard: Old Home Week. My Mother used to take my sisters, and my Father and I would go another day, and I guess we'd just have to go on the bus. We had no vehicle.

Richard: [to Barbara W. Mackenzie] Do you remember Marvin Johnston? I think he owned the bus. And that was the only means we had of getting to Charlottetown.

Tom: The train?

Richard: The train. Well the train was before our time. When we got our first vehicle, we used to load everybody in the back. And we'd go to O'Keefe's Lake and then my Father would take us to the movies at the old theatre. We'd drive in the back of the truck.

Tom: And the regulations about not having seat belts—did you ever lose anybody off the side?

Barbara: Ha Ha. [Regulations] were not in existence at all. But the Provincial Exhibition drew people from all over the Island and it was the best of everything—the best of all the foods—vegetables etc.

Richard: There was no night racing back then.

Barbara: No. No.

Richard: The only way they could get there was by bus—previous to having a vehicle.

Tom: The thing that drives me crazy is that they have these exhibits of produce, but they do it before the crops are ready. I went to the Indiana State Fair and they have this exhibit for apples, but they have it some time in August. So how do you compare *this* set of unripe apples to *that* set of unripe apples? It's months too early.

Barbara: We have the baking, everything from biscuits to pies and cakes and then the pickling.

Then there was the knitting and the quilting. Photography, now, is a new one—but it didn't used to be there. And flower displays—all the different flower displays—needed to be set up and judged. And it would be all printed in the Guardian.

Richard: One of the main attractions back then was the horse races and the livestock show.

Barbara: They used to bring the oxen teams over from Nova Scotia. They were wonderful! They were groomed to perfection and the bells—all done up with bells and the harness—all of the brass.

Activities: Old Home Week

People would enter their pickles and jams for judging. One woman submitted a jar of canned beans every year for about 10 years, and it would always take a prize because it was so pretty, but it was always the same bottle (laughter).

A perfect loaf

Dora: We always had to put something in the Exhibition—we had to sew or knit, darn socks or whatever. One time my sister Ena, her real name was Lorena, made a perfect loaf of bread. She put it at the bottom of the bin, in a safe place she thought. But Pup [our father] always got up first thing in the morning and he reached to the bottom of the bin. Guess what, the loaf was gone, so she had to make another loaf and did get first prize. She was called 'the bread mixer' at school after that.

Picking for admission

dd: When Old Home Week started, Dad (Nelson Buell of Abney) would take us in. We would pick blueberries by the bucket and sell them for money to pay to get in. Dad had a Ford rumble-seat car and as many as could fit piled in.

Horse racing

Richard: Getting back to goin' to The Exhibition, Old Home Week, we used to call it The Exhibition until somebody put that nickname on it in later years. I had four sisters, and Mom and the four sisters used to go one day, because we had a relative that lived right handy to the exhibition grounds, and they used to go there and then they'd go from there to the exhibition. And then my father and I would go another day, and of course we hadda go by bus.

Another thing that used to be quite an attraction was the Vaudeville that they had between the races. That was a big attraction which they don't have anymore. They had high wire acts. They had high acrobat frames or whatever they call them and that was an attraction. Other than that there've been big changes.

I'd just like to comment on the difference in the horse races back then compared to now. My father was very fond of horse races. Back then there

was no starting gate and if they didn't all line up right, they hadda start again—a false start. It wasn't until 1970 possibly that the two-minute-mile was broke. It was broken by Saul's Pride, an Australian horse. Back in our day there was no such thing as a two-minute-mile; it was 2:30, even 3 minutes, so the horses have speeded up. Now there's hardly such a thing as a 2 minute mile.

Tom: This is *harness* racing?

Richard: Yeah, harness racing. Harness racing has a long history on PEI.

Ron: You remember when they used to race in the ice in North River?

Richard: I never saw one.

Ron: Every Saturday.

Tom: Do they have special hooves for the horses—cleats?

Pat(?): Yes they did.

Ron: Cleats, somewhat, I guess you could call them that.

Pat: Sort of clam shoes.

Rides and potato picking

Pat: Old Home Week was the highlight of the year for us.

Tom: Talk to us about old home week, Ron, you haven't said much lately.

Ron: Not much to say—you went and spent the money you had, and that was about it.

Tom: Did they have the rides?

Ron: Yeah, they had a few, Ferris wheel that kind of stuff—nothing like they have now of course.

Pat: You spent all your strawberry-picking money and stuff.

Ron: The cattle, and that kind of stuff. They always had the animals.

Tom: Did you go on the rides?

Ron: Yeah I went on a few. Back then they had potato picking all day. So you saved your money from picking potatoes. They closed the school for 2 weeks. You would pick potatoes and save your money.

Pat: Only on PEI we had potato-picking though.

Ron: 'Potato-picking holidays' you used to call them.

Richard: It was always in August wasn't it, Old Home Week?

Ron: Yes.

Pat: The end of August.

Ron: We always saved it...

Richard: Later in August than it is now.

Pat: The very end. It seems school started right after Old Home Week.

Tom: So you would get off for picking potatoes? Did everybody go pick potatoes or did some of them just have it off.

Pat: We had no way of knowing. We just got the time off and we went and picked.

Ron: Most of the kids who went to the country schools were part of it.

Richard: I have to question on that because Old Home Week would be *over* before we were picking.

Ron: You saved your money from the year before.

Richard: How'd you do that?

Ron: The stores weren't right next door like they are now.

Pat: We used to get paid for picking strawberries--so much a box and we used to save that.

Ron: My aunt and uncle own Balderson's, so we picked strawberries as well.

Tom: You don't get any free vegetables now?

Ron: No. You never got nothing free back then either. They're still 'relatives with the vegetable stand'.

FAIRS

Antique machinery shows

Richard: We'd take [the truck] to shows—Antique Shows.

Richard: They used to be over here—that was a great spot, behind the Shanty. It was a great place—where the Monks are now [in Montague]. In the meantime—someone was going to develop behind there. It never happened. The show moved to Brudenell—which is not as convenient.

Tom: Are there a lot of vehicles that come to these things...I mean from off-Island? Why would they come to PEI to show?

Richard: Pretty near 40 Years coming up.

Tom: 40 Years! So you've been showing nearly 30 years then.

Richard: I've been showing pretty well every year. Another fellow, lives just down the road here, he's been in every one.

Tom: Does it cost much to enter?

Richard: It's a 3 day affair. I only go on Sunday afternoon.

Tom: So you have to pay?

Richard: I have another vehicle too. I put the 2 of them in for about $15. I have another vehicle too but I don't bother—it's too new. Antique vehicles are a big draw now. They have a Tractor Club too, which I belong to. I have an antique tractor too. A '54 Cockshut.

And they have [a tractor show] in Brudenell. There's more than tractors—there's antique machinery and vehicles—the whole bit...

Tom: They have a tractor pull...

Richard: That's something I'm not interested in. Smoke and dust. They have them all souped up.

Tom: Ok. These are not ordinary tractors—this is something that has very little relation to a tractor.

Richard: The Dundas Ploughing Match—does that name ring a bell to you?

Activities: Fairs 65

Tom: I've heard of it.

Richard: They have horse-pulls. They have a building there with machinery. Old, machinery. 1941—Elaine Trac Rennon[?]. There's lots of material there. There are all kinds of pictures.

The last few years, they grow a field of grain, and they cut it with the binder before the ploughing match. Martin MacLeod has a thrasher and he takes the thrasher in and demonstrates the thrasher at the Ploughing Match. So you'll have to go down to that Ploughing Match

Royal (Toronto) Winter Fair

Richard: I had an opportunity to go to Toronto. I used to collect for the Big Brothers, and there was a contest on. At that time people that were canvassing had an opportunity to win a trip to any city in Canada that you choose. I happened to win, and I could take one person with me. So anyway first thing that come to mind was the Royal Winter Fair, being a farmer, and I took my next door neighbour

Pat: Male of female?

Richard: Now, come now! Anyway, it was November, early first or second week, and it was an experience of a lifetime—the Royal Winter Fair. It consists of

10 acres—probably bigger now—and there's entertainment, animals of all species, but the thing that caught my eye was all those people dressed in tuxedos. We were very curious to know why they were dressed to kill. Didn't take me very long to find out why they were dressed—they were at the horse show. Everybody in the audience at the draft horse show was dressed in tuxedos. I couldn't believe it. The harness that was on them horses was unreal. You can get a example when you go to Charlottetown—Old Home Week—but this was a huge—you seen it?

Tina: It's gorgeous.

Richard: Did you see everybody in tuxedos?

Ron: Yes, yes.

Richard: And you were wondering why they were in tuxedos too were you?

Ron: I can't remember wondering—somebody probably pointed it out.

Richard: Who's getting' married? What's going on here?

Pat: This is tradition I suppose.

Richard: But we went in just with what we were wearing. Nobody said anything.

Tina: No they won't as long as you don't get into the area where those guys are with the tuxedos.

Richard: We were right among them. Nobody said anything. How were we supposed to have a tuxedo?

Tom: Do you *have* a tuxedo?

Richard: No way.

Barbara: Have you *ever* had a tuxedo?

Richard: No. Anyway it was the experience of a lifetime.

Ron: Bobby Hall had cattle there and I looked after his cattle. Stay up with them all night and keep them clean because he'd be showin' them the next day. Miss Canada was from PEI that year, so I got them at meet her. I had pictures of her at home.

Tom: She wasn't wearing a tuxedo?

Ron: No, she had on the Island Tartan.

Richard: Getting back to Bobby Hall.

Pat: How did we get to Bobby Hall?

Richard: He had his cattle at the fair. The hotel we stayed at—I went down to

Activities: Fairs

the lobby and I run into the man that was taking care of his cattle. Him and I had a great chat. That's quite a coincidence.

Ron: Yes it is.

Richard: I'm not sure what breed...

Ron: Herefords I believe.

[?]: black and white?

Ron: Just Black Angus. We had dual purpose Shorthorn.

Richard: They're all brown.

Ron: [Hurleys?] had them out in Winsloe.

Richard: There's hardly any of them left now. They were a popular breed one time. I don't think there's one herd on the Island.

Ron: The bull he brought up that year—you couldn't fit it across in the boxcar, we had to put it this way, it was so big. [gesture not recorded] One of the Grand Champion level.

Away to skating contests

Tina: You were also involved with sports?

Peggy: Oh yes. Hockey, anything like that. I didn't play hockey because I didn't have skates, but I done the other sports. When the children started, they all played and I said, "Girls are going to do the same as the boys."

I had 7 children and they all played sports. We lived in Valleyfield then—we came to the Island. We would go up to Montague every day for hockey, wherever there was a hockey game, I was there—any kind of sports—I still would if I could just get there.

Tina: That's nice to keep up with things you like.

Peggy: There was girls and boys playing hockey, they were speed skating and they were doing the other sports—races and stuff—and they traveled a lot. We used to go on trips with them. We always went. The only place that had speed skating was in Montague, so we used to travel to New Brunswick and Quebec and Ontario and around like that to play. So that's what I enjoyed, was stuff like that, so once the children grew up, I was out again.

Holidays

Halloween

Trick or treating

Pat: We were discussing Halloween and of course it was the highlight of our life. We started weeks in advance, planning what we were going to wear and of course we didn't have a lot of money and we didn't have much imagination. We just threw on somebody's old shirt and rubber boots and that kind of thing, but we made a big deal of it. We started around the neighbourhood.

We hit every house—not that there were that many houses—but we did. We hit every house, and in those days homeowners were prepared for us too. There were always wonderful marshmallow balls and cookies and candy and loads of it, and sometimes we'd get asked in to have some punch or something to drink, and in that case we didn't egg their windows or anything. They were being nice to us. But everybody else was treated like that—we egged their windows and tipped over everything we could find and generally made a mess of everything. But it was all sort of part of the fun. There was one particular house we went to and the woman, she was very fond of kids and she always prepared all kinds of wonderful goodies, and at that house we were invited in. Her house was just brimming with kids and we'd bob for apples. She was a wonderful person. Her name was Mrs. Good and she certainly was good, and she loved us all.

Anyway, after we'd done a lot of damage, we had to trudge home with our bags and all our goodies, and mother and sister—we'd dump it all out on the floor so she could inspect it. She would make sure we weren't getting any of that salt water taffy, and then we were good to go.

Tom: What was bad about salt water taffy?

Pat: It was bad for your teeth.

Holidays: Halloween

All: Oh!

Pat: That's pretty much it. Then we longed for Christmas after that, but Halloween was the highlight of our season.

Barbara: I guess when I was a little kid Halloween was a big deal for kids, but it wasn't for the community *per se* because when we dressed up, that amounted to putting on a mask of some kind, a cat mask or something like that, and we couldn't see and we couldn't breathe, but we were allowed to go out and we always waited until dark too. We didn't go in the daylight. And we'd go out and, of course being in a rural area, the farm houses were pretty far apart. All we had was a little brown paper bag—nowadays you see kids with pillowcases and sometimes two or three pillowcases. All we had was a little paper bag. People would give us Halloween kisses which you call salt water taffy. That was pretty well all we got. I remember one year we went out, we were probably about age 7 or 8. It's funny our parents let us roam around the neighbourhood in the dark—three or four of us—and we got to one house and the guy gave us a pencil each! Talk about insulting.

One time we got really, really brave and we went all the way up the road to about a mile past my house. We went, knocked on the door of the house, and the door was partly open, so when we knocked it swung open and it kind of creaked on the way in, and we just stood on the doorstep—and nobody came to the door, but there on the table was a big bowl of candies. We talked to one another. Should we go in? Maybe there's nobody home. Should we take them? Maybe somebody was watching us and would come out and be cross at us. Eventually we wandered in and took a couple of candies each. That was the only time we went up the road.

But the older teenagers in our community—they were a little bit on the bad side because there was always someone in the community you could tease. And those people would come out and make a run for you, and you would run away and it was great fun. One of the people happened to be our next door neighbours—the farm next us. The woman was one of the kindest people you've ever met and the man was very humorous—not a very hard worker but a very humorous little guy, and great friends of Mom and Dad and everybody in the neighbourhood. But they were a target. There'd be probably about 15 or 20 older kids out hooting and hollering and throwing eggs and soaping the windows and calling out, and eventually he'd run out and chase them away, and they'd come back, and they'd keep this up for hours on end.

One night my sister came home—she had been out with her friends—she was really worried, she said, "I lost my scarf."

"Well you can get it tomorrow. When it's daylight, you'll see where it is."

"Yeah, but I lost it at our next door neighbour's."

So she was one of the gang—dead giveaway. So the next morning Dad said, "Down you go."

And she went and didn't find her scarf. She went into the house and talked to the lady there. They were both telling her about all these bad, bad children who had come annoying them.

Doris (my sister) was saying, "Oh, I'm so sorry! Really that was too bad." and she sympathizing all over the place.

Eventually on the way home she found where she had dropped her scarf and picked it up and came home. That was Halloween back then. I don't think kids enjoy it as much today as they did back then. It's just a candy hunt now, but we always had trick or treat and we had our bar of soap with us. If someone was rather mean they got the soap on the window. We got our share at our house as well. There's my story.

Ghost arising in the cemetery

Miriam: We used to go to young people's [church meeting] in Belfast. One evening we had a corn boil and Ed White was his name—he was a kind of a funny fella and was always playing tricks—anyway he came over to the boil up around the cemetery—came up out of the cemetery and we thought there was somebody that was dead came alive—scared the living heart out of us!

Creating a haunted house legend

Pat: We're going to talk about hauntings and graveyards and anything that's scary. I'd like to start with the year we bought the old house down in Lower Montague. Now this old house had been abandoned and was reputed to be haunted. It was right at the end of the road at the time, and right across from Georgetown, so the lights from Georgetown on certain nights would ripple across the water and be picked up by the upstairs windows in this old house and that gave the title of haunted; everybody knew it was haunted because there were lights upstairs. I heard about this house, and my husband was getting ready to retire, so we bought it and spent lots of time fixing it up. As soon as my children started to school they were told, "You're living in a haunted house."

Well they came home from school and said, "Mom this house is haunted."

And so I said, "Oh is that right. Well maybe we can do something about that."

I knew this was the friendliest house in the world, because when we came to look at it just welcomed me and said, "Come in." So I knew it wasn't haunted. They were so concerned about it so I thought, "We're going to make some book with this."

So I said, "Well, we'll tell everybody it's haunted and you can go to school and tell them all these horror stories."

The first horror story was the fact that we bought the house from some people who lived in Boston and their name was Westaway. Everybody knew the old house was 'the Westaway house'. These people had trouble getting back and forth to the Island, so they sold the house. So we decided we'd make something out of that. I'd heard a story about the original Westaway, and how he had died, and the manner in which he had died. I made this all up out of my head, although there was some truth to it, that the man had died during a very bad winter storm—Roger Westaway—I think that was his name. He happened to die during the winter storm and his wife at the time had to find somebody to sign a kind of a death certificate. At that time anybody who had any kind of important job could sign it, so they happened to be ploughing the road at the time. She went down to the road and asked the supervisor if he would come up and say that Roger was dead and sign a piece of paper, which he did. After the thaw, they put Roger on a ferry— there was a ferry over to Georgetown—so he was put on the ferry, taken over to Georgetown and buried with quite a lot of ceremony and that was fine. Well, word got to his sister that lived in Boston that he had died. Word was very slow getting to Boston in those days. She got rather uppity about it and decided that the widow had poisoned Roger. She was so adamant about this that they were forced to exhume Roger from Georgetown, put him on a train and send him to Montreal where the forensics unit was. Okay, poor old Roger got sent up there and after a little while he got sent back again on the train because he was obviously not poisoned and it was an ordinary death.

So poor old Roger got taken over to Georgetown and buried for the second time.

When I heard this story I thought, 'This is fun, we can make up something about how he is haunting this house because he got bumped down the stairs, unceremoniously dumped on the bottom, and taken over to Georgetown on this little ferry and he was very unhappy about that.'

I said to the children, "You can tell the kids at school this," which they did.

Then of course I started making up other things and it sort of backfired on me because every time there was a noise, or something making a noise in the attic, I had to come up with a story for it. So of course we had bats; as soon as we moved in the bats came down from the attic and swarmed around, and we just sort of had to hunch down and wait for them to go out the back door. The next day my son went up and fixed the attic door so bats wouldn't get out. Anyway, we had bats.

Then one night there was a violent windstorm my daughter came flying into my bedroom and she said, "Mom, something is making a howling noise in my bedroom."

So I said, "Okay."

I got up out of bed, went to her room, stood there a few minutes. Sure enough there was this awful moaning noise. I thought to myself, 'Hmmm, nothing I can do about that.' So she came and got into bed with me and eventually went to sleep. The next morning I was forced to find the source of this moaning. I couldn't find anything in the room, went up to the attic, nothing there, went outside, cruised around looking outside and sure enough the wind had dislodged a downspout from the gutter, and the wind blowing over the top of the downspout made this howling noise. Alright we got that one sorted out. Yes. My son fixed that.

During the summer we had lots of blow flies and mosquitoes—we had everything that year. The poor old house had suffered.

Just before bedtime my son came flying up and said, "There's an awful noise in my bedroom."

I thought, 'Here we go again.'

So I go up in his bedroom and I could hear this noise and it was a real flapping noise. I stayed there for a few minutes and I went down and looked at everything and it was coming from a poster that was on his bedroom wall and one of these great big old blow flies had got behind the poster and was making this terrible buzzing noise. Okay, so I picked up the fly swatter and I whacked the poster. Another ghost taken care of.

Tom: What you call a blow fly—is that what we call a shingle fly or cluster fly?

Pat: Yes and of course our house being so old, there was a lot of those shingle flies because the shingles were kind of getting loose and they'd get behind.

So that was the tale of the haunted house that wasn't really haunted and it's still standing there today. It's the quietest house. You go there and sleep down there—there's not a sound. It's very peaceful. And that's the house that finally got the family it deserved and it's happy.

Barbara: Been there myself.

Bump in the night

Tom: I don't have any haunting stories but I do have a story about 'things that go [something] in the night'. My wife and I were living in a house while we were remodelling it. Somewhere in the middle of the night there is this flapping, flapping, flapping and I just pull the covers over my head and said, "Don't worry about it it's just a bird. I'll get it out in the morning." And she says, "Birds don't fly at night." And it was a bat. I'm not a big on smashing bats. We generally just open a window and eventually it will be gone. There's not much shelter for bats around anyway, and they're good.

CHRISTMAS

Homemade decorations

Peggy: I used to draw, like for Christmas. You didn't buy decorations; we made everything ourselves. On the Christmas tree and we decorated it.

Tina: We did too.

Peggy: We'd go to the woods and get the tree and put it up, and get the stuff fixed up all around the windows and everything like that. It was just the way we lived.

A big thing at Christmas: we hoped to get an apple or an orange for

Christmas. That was the only thing we got. The big thing about Christmas was midnight mass. We'd go to church in the evening and we'd go to Fort Hood and the stores there would be open. We could go in there before we went to church—just stuff like that when we were kids—kind of different than it is today.

Presents

Ethel: I remember one Christmas in the 1930s getting a toy watch, scribbler, pencils and an eraser plus one orange and apple each from Santa Claus—and happy to get them. We all went downstairs together to see if Santa came.

Stockings

Mary Ellen: We had Christmas concerts in the school.

In our stockings would be an apple, an orange, hard candy, pencils, and crayons, all of which we were glad to get.

Santa Claus, presents, and kindness

Winnie: I can remember when I first found out there was no Santa Claus. I had a coat and bonnet that matched that someone had sent me from the States. I was getting ready to go to church and they sent me into the guest room—the spare room—to get my coat and hat. When I took my coat off the bed, the blanket moved and I saw, underneath the blanket, the doll that I was wanting for Christmas. I think I was nine—eight or nine—because when I asked my Mom, she said, "Well, no really there is no such thing as Santa Claus, but keep quiet about it so you won't spoil it for the younger children."

Tom: How many children were you?

Winnie: There was seven of us at that time, I think.

Then we moved to Bear River and my mother got sick. She was in the hospital over Christmas. The big thing for Christmas was they sent an order to Eaton's and each child knew you were allowed one gift and so you'd say what you wanted. If you were lucky you got it, and if you weren't, you didn't!

Holidays: Christmas

But Mother had done this earlier on, but they left the gifts out in Rollo Bay at Grandma's house. It was stormy and Dad then drove on horseback from Bear River to Rollo Bay to get our Christmas presents, and brought them home to Bear River. While he was gone my brother and I—they used to put banking around the house, this was before...

Tom: Insulation?

Winnie: That's it. Usually in some places—I think Murray River and Murray Harbour—they used seaweed. In some places they use hay bales. In our area that used clay, and then on top of the clay they usually put some little evergreen trees on top of that just to break the wind to keep the draft out of the house. Anyway my brother and I went out and took one of these little trees off the banking and we brought it in the house, and Grandma—we tried to make it stand up; we didn't have a stand or anything—and Grandma showed us how to put a nail in the corners and put a string around it and then tie the strings onto these nails to hold it steady. We had a box with old ornaments from other years, and so we got the thing up and we had Christmas, on top of which some of the neighbour ladies—I believe it was the Women's Institute—had gotten together, and they came to the house with baking, and cookies, and cake, and even a stuffed chicken. We ate like kings for the rest of the week or a week or so. Often people have said to me how I'm usually wanting to do things for other people or being involved in community, and it always goes back—in my mind it always goes back to how people were so good to us, and if there is anything I can do to help anyone else, then I'm willing to do it.

Winnie: The last Christmas that I'll tell you about is one a few years later. I was the oldest, so I got the job of writing the order for Christmas. My one sister wanted a shoulder purse, one wanted skates, my oldest brother wanted a Swiss Army knife. I can't remember—someone else wanted a wallet, the two younger ones wanted—the girls wanted a monkey—there were stuffed monkeys and for some reason she wanted this monkey, and the younger one wanted a little teddy bear that was blue and pink. I can still see it. My greatest wish was for a little camera—a little Brownie camera. My girlfriends had one and they were willing to share their pictures with me, but I dearly wanted one of my own. Anyway, off the order went, and when it came back everything was in it except for the camera. I told Daddy, "Everything is fine. Don't worry. (I was 17 or 16 at the time) I can get along without it."

Christmas morning came and we got up, and the children opened their gifts and we were having hot chocolate or something, and Dad sent my brother out to the barn to bring in the parcel that was out there on a beam and when he came in, I was presented with this parcel, and there was my Brownie camera. [sniffles] Dad had got it at the drugstore in Souris, and I had that camera 'til after I was married. The first pictures of my older children were taken with that camera. One day my little boy dropped it in the dishpan and that was the end of the camera.

School Christmas concert

Ethel: Our one room schoolhouse was preparing for a Christmas concert. We practiced Jingle Bells for weeks before it was held. There was no music—just the teacher helping us to sing with no other help. The night of the concert the school was a magical place. We opened the concert standing in the front (the teacher's desk had been moved aside). The schoolhouse was packed with parents—standing along the walls. We did our thing including singing and recitations, and then we heard a noise outside and everyone knew it must be Santa. No red suits back then—just the long white beard and an old coat, and probably rubber boots. Santa passed out pencils, pencil boxes, scribblers, oranges and apples to all the children—such an exciting evening that happened each and every year!

Tree for the kittens

Corena: I remember going with my Dad to get the Christmas tree on our farm—a go back in the woods somewhere he'd cut this tree and one time—I do remember—we each had a cat, my brother and I, because my aunt, who lived close to us—her cat had kittens. We probably drove the women crazy goin' every day to see if we could take the kittens. She said we could each have one. We went every day until finally it was time to take the kittens home. We put up this little tree for the kittens [laughter] I'm sure they appreciated it. Just a little, small tree. Dear knows what we decorated it with, but we found something.

Tom: Any idea how old you were?

Corena: Trying to think—probably 6 or 7. We each got a kitten, you know, so that was a big deal. And fruit we used to get in the stocking, with an orange—didn't get that very much—and maybe there would be an apple in there too, and probably some candies. That was what was in your stocking.

[?]: And maybe a hair ribbon or a barrette—a comb or something for the boys.

Corena: Just small things. My uncle, I was thinking about the order—when you talk about the order going in for Christmas—my uncle—my mother's Mom had one brother that had lost part of his leg in a farm accident. He delivered our mail. He delivered it in horse and wagon, and horse and sleigh in the winter. Anyway, we lived close to the end of the road, and he would stop when he got to our place for a hot lunch. It would be like a dinner meal. Mom would always have a hot meal for him, and he always spent Christmas with us. He had never married, and he spent Christmas with us. When Mom would send an order at Christmas time, Simpson's or whatever, he paid for that. That was compensation for the hot meal that Mom provided for him.

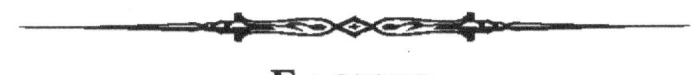

EASTER

Holy Week for a Catholic

Tom: I wonder if you could describe what Good Friday through Easter was like with your Catholic background, and what you did, and so on.

Winnie: Yes, Easter.... Holy Thursday was the beginning of Holy Week, and it commemorates Jesus—the Blessed Sacrament. Jesus at the Last Supper left His body and blood for the people—can't think of the word. At any rate that was—it wasn't a holy day of obligation, but we always went to church on Holy Thursday, and after Mass was over, the priest and the altar boys took all the altar cloths and everything took them all away and bared the altar altogether.

Then for Good Friday there was Mass but there was no Eucharist—we didn't receive Eucharist, and there was what they called Veneration of the Cross. They had a big cross at the front of the church and first the priest prostrated himself to the cross and the cross was laid on the steps going up to the Altar and he kissed the cross, then the older boys did it, and then the general congregation did it. I'm not sure if there was a reading—there must have been, but I can't remember. We still do something similar now, but we have the cross standing up and we touch it with our fingers or whatever—Venerate the Cross at any rate. The Passion was read—the Passion of Jesus—the agony in the garden and all that. That was read for that service, and then we left the church quietly and went home.

Holy Saturday started with—it still does—the Blessing of the New Fire. They made a fire from the palms from last year's Palm Sunday.

Tom: Oh, a year ago.

Winnie: No, maybe it was from the same year. At any rate, they burn the palm, and this was the lighting of the new fire—a new beginning because now Jesus is risen from the dead. They bless the holy water for the following year. It's a long service.

Tom: On Saturday?

Winnie: Yes.

Tom: I didn't even know there was a *Saturday* activity.

Winnie: Oh yes. The catechumens—the people who had taken instructions to become Catholic—were baptized at that time with the new holy water.

Tom: These were people who were becoming Catholics as adults? Infants wouldn't do that.

Winnie: No, no, no. We baptize children when they are infants in the Catholic religion. Yes. No these were adults who were becoming Catholics.

Tom: My Protestant bias is showing. I'll let you keep going.

Winnie: Easter morning, we went to Mass as usual. A lot of singing: *Glory Alleluia*—a glorious occasion. The priest was dressed in white vestments, which would not normally be, and then at home everybody could have an egg or *two* eggs for breakfast. We didn't know anything about the Easter Bunny. We never heard tell about that. Grandma used to try to have a new hat, or at least put a new ribbon on one she already had, or put a rose on one, or a flower of some sort (an artificial one, of course) instead of the normal feather, because it was Easter.

Tom: So dressing up consisted of changing her hat.

Winnie: Yes, lucky if she was able to do that. At that point in time—this was in 1940 something.

Tom: We're not talking your mother, you said grandmother. Was your mother with you at that time?

Winnie: Because she had always had a small child, often she didn't come to church, and Dad was always there because he sang in the choir, and his father played the organ, and his sister played the organ.

Tom: So Easter was a big time.

Winnie: Yes, a big celebration.

Tom: Yes, even Protestants do that. Well, thank you.

CANADA DAY

Origins

Tom: Let's talk about Canada day since that was yesterday. First of all tell us what you did to celebrate it yesterday, if anything, and then try to remember Canada days from long ago.

[?]: Did we celebrate…?

Richard: Very, very little.

Ron: I don't remember celebrating either. It wasn't the big fuss made back when we were little.

Tom: So long ago Canada Day….

Tina: I went to school and we sang *Oh Canada* and that was it.

Pat: I think Old Home Week is something that we would remember more about.

Richard: It's only come in about 10 years ago. Never a big deal.

Tom: Well, coming from the States, I consider it a poor imitation for the 4th of July.

Pat: No we never celebrated—I don't ever remember…

Richard: No great memories of Canada Day. I don't even know if they called it 'Canada Day'.

Tina: I remember Canada Day after I was married and living in Ontario. Ottawa started with the fair that they had for Canada Day and the RCMP Rides—that was started for Canada Day.

Tom: The horse show?

Tina: That's when I first remember Canada Day. The first year we lived there we had a booth at the fair for the company that we worked for. We were at the fair. The evening we had off, so we went and on the rides if we wanted to—just my husband and myself.

Tom: So did you go on rides?

Tina: Yes we went on some.

Tom: What did you go on?

Tina: Oh, just the Ferris wheel and—what do they call it? Snake? The roller coaster.

Tom: They had a roller-coaster?

Tina: The small one—not a big one. Any of the other type of rides you wouldn't catch me on—except maybe for the children's horsey ride. My brother was visiting and he had his little ones, so I'd go with one or two of them, one on each horse, and he do the same thing with the other ones. So that's how we ended up at the fair on Canada Day. That's when I remember Canada Day

Tom: Sounds sad that kids have to ride on a horse as a special thing, after the way it was when you were young, I imagine.

Tina: Well, yeah, my daughter, when she was young, we had actually a racing mare, Lindsay Dollard. There was only one fella that could handle her, he was a young fellow that worked for us, and he would put my daughter—first time I saw her on the back of that horse I just about had kittens. I was terrified.

He looked at me, he said, "She's fine."

He was walking beside her. He was leading the horse but he was staying right beside. Her he held on to the horse's harness and he walked with her. We even took this horse over to the church [next door]. We took four horses over to the church and gave kids rides at the church for their Canada Day, which was enjoyed. Nobody had to pay a penny to go on the rides, which is different from today.

Anyway, you see a horse, "Oh, can I go for a ride?" Money first—then you go for a ride.

That's was how we ended up that summer. The only thing I got out of that day at the church and the school parade was a bad burn on the back of my neck. That was from holding the horse and the child at the same time while we were taking them around.

True North

Tom: I have a question for all of you native Canadians. How long has *O Canada* been the anthem? All of your life?

Tina: Ever since I started school.

Tom: OK, a very long time. The US switched from *My Country Tis of Thee* to the *Star Spangled Banner.* But a question I have is, "What on Earth is 'the true north'?"

Pat: *We're* the true north.

Tom: We are the true north? So all of Canada is the true north? I thought it had something to do with the Inuit or something.

[various]: No!

Tina: We were the true north before the Inuit even [became part of] Canada.

Tom: Okay.

Pat: We've cleared that up. Remember *we're* the true north.

Tom: Well I'm part of it now too. We're citizens now.

Tina: We've adopted you.

Tom: Well, you see, I was old enough that I didn't have to pass the test on Canadian history, fortunately. They said, "Well old people can't learn this stuff," I guess.

Tina: Take the two sixteen-year-olds that I told you about. I was their age and they thought Canada was Ontario and Quebec.

Ron: To be fair, they didn't teach a lot of Canadian history when we went to school. It was more about the United States and other countries.

Tom: Really!

Pat: British history was very big, wasn't it? We learned dates about the battles, and King Henry and all that kind of [stuff].

Tina: Anyone from Manitoba, Saskatchewan, or Alberta—they had Canada down pat—they knew about all the provinces. From Manitoba this way they didn't—a least Ontario didn't seem to.

Tom: Well, they counted everything that was important right?

Tina: Ontario should have been important as well as the rest.

Tom: I mean the West—that's not important.

Tina: Well the West was not important to just teens in the rest of the country.

MEMORABLE EVENTS

WARS

Knitting for the troops

Ruth: My grandmother loved spinning and weaving as well as knitting and working yarns to make very pretty patterns of sweaters. She did a lot of knitting for the men who went overseas to WW I from 1914 to 1918. She often wondered if those mittens and socks ever reached their destinations. Transportation was mostly by boat. It was not always sure when or where parcels were stored until passage was available.

News and letters were few and far between. Word from relatives and friends serving overseas was eagerly awaited. Most news of anyone killed or injured was heard through the railway codes that came into the train stations, but notices were sent out by mail or sometimes a footman from a certain regiment would deliver the news to families. After the war ended many soldiers came back to the Island but some moved to central or western Canada and some took up residence in Maine or New Hampshire, where the pulp mills were prospering.

War evacuee to Canada

Pat: My story starts in London, England in 1940. War had been declared and London was bombed nightly. My sister, Doris and I were aged nine and eleven. My father had been called up for active duty. Children were being evacuated from London and my father requested that we also were to be removed from harm's way. My mother applied and we were accepted, not knowing where we were to be located. Soon we were on our way by train to Liverpool and were housed for the night in a large warehouse with dozens of cots. This was the first time in our lives that we had been separated from our mother and tears flowed as I realized that I might not see her again for a long while. My sister tried to comfort me as best she could. In the morning we were bussed to the dock, where this enormous ship was docked, along with many others waiting to depart. Can you imagine the amazement of a bunch of cocky little London kids? Most had never seen the ocean, and certainly never seen an ocean liner.

Soon we were boarding. We were divided into groups of twelve and placed in the care of the Salvation Army lassies complete with bonnets and black dresses. This should have been intimidating, but we were so full of wonder that we tore about this ship, gawking at everything and getting in the crews' way. The ship sailed at night. When we woke there was no sight of land, only other ships in convoy, protected from German submarines by destroyers.

I remember the voyage as a very pleasant trip, and for ten days we made new friends, the boys fought with each other and kept the crew busy attempting to keep them out of sensitive areas. Eventually Halifax harbour came into view. As soon as we docked, we were divided into groups going to different provinces across Canada. My sister and I were put on a train bound for PEI. with 25 others. Word spread before us and as the train stopped at towns across Nova Scotia, the local people hurried down to the stations to see these strange kids from a foreign land; they handed in ice cream cones and chocolate bars, and treated us like celebrities. I remember the train went straight to the ferry. When we arrived in Charlottetown in the evening we were taken to a farm and put in quarantine for several days and tested for all kinds of things.

Soon the big day arrived and prospective foster parents began checking us out; most wanted boys to replace the farm hands who had enlisted in the forces, but luck was with us and we were introduced to our new parents, Jack and Belle MacLeod, who took us to their farm on North River Road. They ran a market garden and sold directly to the stores in town. I immediately fell in love with the whole thing and wanted to help with chickens and the cows and picking corn, which was just coming to harvest.

I spent my 10th birthday surrounded by dozens of people who showed up for the publicity, including the premier of PEI. My foster mother was overwhelmed, particularly as she didn't vote for him or even like him.

School started and I was enrolled in Spring Park School where I again made a lot of new friends. The next five years followed with happiness and love and new experiences. I learned to skate and swim in the North River; I joined Girl Guides and went camping. I picked strawberries and potatoes and turned into a gawky teenager. I sang in the junior choir at Zion Presbyterian Church and had a few boyfriends as well.

But eventually this idyllic phase of my life ended, and we were once again headed for the train for Halifax. A sad bunch of teenagers filled the ship and headed back to parents we scarcely remembered. When the ship docked in Southampton we were put on a train to London where dozens of parents waited—of course they were not expecting teenagers, and sorting out took a while. When there were only two mothers left, my sister and I had to decide which was ours, so we waited until she decided. I can't say it was a joyful reunion. We headed back to our old home, but it appeared cramped compared to our large bedroom in Charlottetown, and we wondered what we were supposed to do with ourselves next. My father arrived home from the Far East and to us girls he looked like the handsomest man we had ever seen, with his dark tan and officers' uniform. He quickly sized up the situation and soon bought a house in a small country village peopled by strange-talking types, whom we couldn't understand, but they treated us kindly and we settled in again.

> [Pat went on to outline getting a job, getting married, returning to Canada, having children, and her moves over the next 60 years before she came to her present place on PEI.]

War brides

Arlene: But [Dad] was gassed in Ypres. So he was taken to the hospital and that's where he met Mom."

Dora: Was she a nurse?

Arlene: Yes, in Manchester. And her Mom didn't want her to leave, to go to Canada.

But I remember hearing Mom say that when they came to Canada, the whole ship would be loaded with return men and the ones that they'd married over there. And some of them kept in touch. Some that went—especially to Saskatchewan—returned to England. They couldn't take it.

Mary: It would be so different.

Arlene: You don't have any close neighbours in Saskatchewan. And a lot of them, they didn't tell their wives what it was like. And they came to something like that?

Dora: It'd be an awful shame, wouldn't it?

Arlene: They just left and went back.

> [A quiet silence spread through the room as we reflected over our conversation.]

German doctor

Arlene: [My brother] Jack—well, John but he was called Jack—used to deliver papers when he was younger and he worked at the theatre. Then there was three years between them, was my sister Susan, but my father nicknamed her 'Toots'. I wasn't as close to my brother as to my sister. We were as we got older. As soon as the war broke out—the Second World War—my brother joined up. There were a lot of years that I didn't see him. Then, when he came home, he lived in Ottawa for quite a few years.

My sister married a chap from the country—he was a teacher, and they didn't get married 'til after the war. But he was a prisoner of war for four years. He was in the air force and was shot down. He needed surgery and the German doctor operated on him and did a wonderful job and he spoke perfect English. Then Toots met him after. They lived in Kincardine and then they moved to St. Catherine's. Then after he retired they moved back to Kincardine.

Blackouts

Neil: An incident comes to mind while World War II was going on. My father, Carl Brydon, and my mother were caretakers on a large estate. He was the farmer and she was the cook. He would run the farm during the day and work at night. Every so often, they used to practice 'blackouts' during the war years. During blackouts, you used to have to cover all the windows and stay inside. This was so that any enemy aircraft flying overhead would not see lights from the home, know there were houses below, and bomb them. There were wardens appointed for the areas, and they would come around to make sure everyone complied with the blackouts. If they knocked on the door looking for my father, they were told that he was working in the barn. This was never questioned; but the fact was that he wasn't in the barn. He had sneaked away through the back fields so that he could drive to work!

Disasters

Chimney fire

Mary: [my own early memories] We had a fire in the house. It was a chimney fire. It was in the spring because there was still some snow and I can remember Mom and my oldest brother, Stephen, getting us all out the back door and either Stephen or Mom went back in to use the telephone which was on the back wall where the old wood stove was. I was terrified because he was so close to the fire.

And we were all standing out by the driveway, shivering, as some of us only had our pyjamas on, and we were pretty ragged looking, and for some reason I looked at Mom and said 'Are we poor?'

I don't remember if it was because we had a wood stove while everyone else had electric stoves, or that we were so ragged looking when the firemen came, but she said, 'We're the poorest ones in this neighbourhood!"

The house I'd been brought up in had been a stately two story, a large house when it had been built in the 1910's.

My grandfather had been a hockey star. He was another John who was called Jack, Twaddle which is a Welsh name. He came from London, Ontario. He had been playing hockey up there and when he moved to Amherst to marry my grandmother, they built the house I grew up in.

There's a big veranda on the front. You go in and there are two big rooms on either side of the front entryway and the stairs go up. There's a big dining room, kitchen and pantry and a little den. And then there are five big bedrooms upstairs. It's a huge old house. I think the only reason we were in it was because they had inherited it. Dad was driving a Coke truck at the time, and delivering Coke-a-Cola, making $50 a week, having a wife and eight kids at home. That would have been the late 50's or 60's."

Arlene: That's not much!

Seeing the Hindenburg

Sister Therese: [written August, 2003] Ever think how you learned to talk? The Royal Bank advertises itself 'One customer at a time'—in learning to talk it's 'one word at a time'. Do you remember the first word you understood? I do!!!!! Know what it was? Rum runner! Strange expression! And maybe at your age and level of English, you may not even know what it means. Let me tell you....

My childhood years were spent at my ancestral home on Panmure Island—near the lighthouse. I think possibly my great grandfather donated—not likely sold—the land to the federal government; the property where this beacon, used by ships and later airplanes, for more than a hundred years, still stands.

My paternal grandfather, William Albert Macdonald, was the keeper of this light during the 1920's and 1930's. He lived with his second wife, affectionately known by her husband's grandchildren as Maggie, in the house provided for the lightkeeper. However he spent a lot of time in my home, which had also been his birthplace and residence for sixty years or more. In his spare time, he helped my father with the farm work, but always with an eye on the sky and the sea, in case a quick storm would be coming up or a pea soup fog was moving in. Like all little girls, GrandDad was a favourite, and even from my baby days I listened for his words of wisdom.

You may wonder what a lightkeeper's job description was in 1930. GrandDad, with his assistant, Matt Condon, shared a seven day week, twenty four hour duty. One of them, usually William, lit the light daily at sundown and Matt's contribution was extinguishing it at sunrise, with hourly checks that it was revolving. Each lighthouse had a distinguishing flash, so the ship's pilots, in the sameness of the sea, knew their location—Panmure's signal was one long flash and one short one. The lighthouse tower was constructed so this would happen. These federal employees also staffed and cared for the machines which put the fog horn in action, to blast out every two minutes a loud, weird sound. This served as a warning to the captains during thick fog or a snowstorm that they were near land. At that time, ship's charts did not show what we now call 'the beach' and fearless seamen have been known to try a short cut to Georgetown, by this route. They went aground and often were wrecked on the shore of the beach. William and

Memorable Events: Disasters

Matt took their responsibilities seriously and valued their work, which put a monthly cheque in their mailboxes—an envied appearance to their neighbours.

While the sun lowered in the western sky, GrandDad climbed the four flights of the white painted, red-towered lighthouse. The first three were more or less rough wooden stairs but the fourth one was a steep steel ladder. Arriving at the top, the climbers pulled themselves up with their arms into the lantern area. The Aladdin lamp with its ashen mantle was lit. The lamp stand was attached to a long steel wire with a heavy base of the same material. The wire was wound onto a large spool, by cranking it up. Then it slowly inched its way down to the building's floor as the light revolved. In summer due to the short nights, one cranking served. However when the nights were long in October or so, at midnight, these devoted men had to climb up and rewind it. The light was not used in January, February and March, as there was no sea travel during these months. There was no electricity on Panmure at this time so they used a hand lantern to illuminate the stairs in the pitch darkness. It was a treacherous climb, but I never heard of a fall.

As well, they watched day and night for thick fog moving in or a snowstorm blowing up. Then the fog horn duties were on. The long, rhythmic blast I'm sure echoed in my foetal consciousness: loud noises have never been big with me.

Supplies for the upkeep of these two valuable signals came yearly by the Government ship which anchored a distance from the beach and the needs brought in by dory. This arrival was a big day, much talked of and anticipated.

I'm not sure if it was a duty assigned to him or his innate commitment to the

Government, but he was frequently spying the ocean for ships that may have been using our waters for illegal purposes. He had a two-foot-long spyglass that one looked into with one eye closed. This brought quite distant objects amazingly clear and seemingly close to the viewer. The illegal seamen, commonly sailing by, were the 'rum runners'. They carried rum and maybe wine from the West Indies or St. Pierre. They often tried to drop their cargo off clandestinely on Prince Edward Island beaches, as far as possible from the watching eye of the police. This kept the price down as it avoided the taxes charged on such goods. GrandDad's sharp eye, however, was probably known, not to be, an easy challenge

He used the word 'rum runners' so often in our kitchen as he told us his experiences with seeing and reporting them. Somehow its musical sound fell on my awakening brain, and for me they are the first words I remember. At this tender age, I didn't know their meaning, but I loved that sound, 'rum runners'.

Radio waves entered the air, and the lightkeepers were given a new responsibility. A two-way radio was installed and William was given a daily hour to turn it on and listen for instructions from headquarters, possibly Charlottetown. He also reported any observations or worries he might have, as he dutifully scanned the seas for ships or for approaching storms. The friendly man on the other end would ask him about his health and that of his family and of course GrandDad returned a similar inquiry. After each bit of conversation, the speaker closed with the word, 'over',

After scanning the seas for years with his famous spyglass, air travel was becoming a reality and new duties were added. In the mid-thirties, he was expected to scan the skies.

At the end of April, 1937, there was big international news. Germany had an airship, the *Hindenburg* being launched on a transatlantic flight to Lakehurst, New Jersey. As people who made such trips in this era did were accustomed to luxury liners, the new mode of travel was built to accommodate fifty passengers in the utmost of comfort. They didn't want nor imagine crossing the ocean, sitting up eating a bag of peanuts and a box lunch. They had chefs, white linen tablecloths in dining rooms with gourmet food and drinks. This maiden voyage was a honoured and privileged occasion for the chosen ones.

About the first of May, 1937, I was thinking about how I would be celebrating my tenth birthday, when GrandDad, normally not an excitable

man, roared into the kitchen shouting, "Quick, outside everyone, the Hindenburg is passing over." So all the family, Daddy, Mom, Andy, Bill, Eddie and I rushed out. I was familiar with seeing the sun and the moon rising in the eastern sky, but now crossing the horizon was what looked like an enormous, oval shaped, grey object—the *Hindenburg*. One-by-one, GrandDad allowed us to close one eye and peep through the famous spyglass as this amazing phenomena passed slowly from our vision.

A few, hours later, as the *Hindenburg's* first passengers were toasting their first view of the USA and chatting with each other about their famous flight, flames broke out and it became air travel's first major disaster. Despite the tragedy, when I hear its name or see the movie on TV, May 6, 1937 brings with it a fond memory of my Panmure Island childhood.

Elections

Honest politicians

Tom: Here you go, for the book, what do you remember about political scandals?

Richard: We had honest politicians back in our day.

Tom: What!

Richard: Yes, they were honest politicians. Our provincial politicians they were all pretty straightforward. There was Walter Jones and Walter Shaw—they were all honest premiers. There wasn't much upheaval back then. And federally we had outstanding prime ministers—we had Diefenbaker and we had Louis St. Laurent and they were all honest politicians. Diefenbaker, he got carried away at the last of it—he got too self-centered. We mostly had liberal, unfortunately, but there wasn't very much scandal.

Tom: My impression of Canadian politics is there a sort of Good Old Boy network and once you're in you're in, and people just don't vote for change.

Richard: Especially on PEI—the narrow-mindedest people in the country. On election day, they don't vote for the party, they vote for the individual. We have a fellow here is running since 1988, MacAuley. They vote him in every time. He has no clout now whatsoever. But there's nobody of note is going to run against him in the next election. So its a shoe-in, and the liberals are in last place after the last election—they only had 33 seats in Ottawa. The NDP is way ahead of them and the Conservatives—well, if you call them conservatives—they're not very conservative. The old conservatives were Progressive Conservatives. That was back in the days of Diefenbaker and previous prime ministers, but now, when Harper came along, they kind of merged with the Tories. Grit is another word for Conservative.

Tom: Long ago I saw that in the *Anne of Green Gables* movie.

Election day

Richard: I'll give you an example of election day—the difference back then. In order to get your vote—nobody had a vehicle—people would volunteer or were hired—I don't know if they got paid. In order to get your vote they'd offer you a pint—of whiskey or rum or whatever. This was how they got your vote.

Tom: Wasn't that illegal?

Richard: Not back then. Everybody was waiting for their pint before they go to the poll. That's a big change.

Tom: They don't give out pints anymore? I assume you'd get in trouble now.

Richard: And the district was divided. One side of the road would vote in a certain location and the other side of the road would have to go to another location. It still is, I guess.

[background voice]: You guys want something to eat?

Richard: If I'd known that I wouldn't have went to McDonald's.

There was one story I could tell you. This man was very witty. He was known for his wit. He always had an answer. So he was going to vote in Cardigan that was his polling place. This fellow was coming out or going into poll.

Somebody said to him, "I wonder what way the [other fellow (?)] will vote."

"He's a grit and a dirty one," he said.

And they'd get feeling pretty good before the votes were all counted. They had people appointed to pick the voters up. Very few people had a vehicle back then. I don't think they went on horses in my day. But I remember people calling for my parents. By the time I got old enough to vote we had a vehicle, but previous to that people were appointed to take you to the poll. They pretty well knew what way you were voting before they took you. There was a driver for the Liberals, and there was a driver for the Conservatives. You weren't assured when you did give them a pint that they would vote for you. You wouldn't actually know.

Political parties and Confederation

Richard: Basically back in our day there was just the two parties the Liberals and the Conservatives. The NDP didn't come in until the late '80s or early '90s when they had candidates. We did elect one NDP—a doctor, Herb Dickinson. He was a good politician and this past election we have a green party, Kevin Baker is his name, but basically it's Tory and Liberal.

[discussion of modern politics omitted]

When everybody joined Confederation—10 provinces joined—that formed Canada.

Tom: PEI was the last [except Newfoundland]. But of the original group, PEI had the confederation meeting, and they didn't vote for it until, what, a decade later?

Richard: That's something I could never understand, why they come across in a boat way back then. There was no ferry or nothing. They come across in some sort of a rowboat. Why would they meet on PEI of all places? That's where Confederation originated. Charlottetown—eighteen fifty something. We had our Centennial. It made history. Why? I have no idea.

Tom: It gave them something to put on license plates.

TRANSPORTATION

HORSES

Jack the triumphant horse

Pat: Growing up on a farm just outside of Charlottetown: We had a mixed garden farm. I got used to all the wonderful animals especially when the cat had kittens. When she scrambled around in the box, you knew there were kittens out there. But the main creature on the farm was the horse. He reigned supreme. He pulled the wagon. He did the ploughing and the harrowing. In the winter, we had an old box sleigh and he drove us back and forth in this old box sleigh. This horse was named Jack. Jack was a mean horse. Jack didn't like anybody—especially me. My job on the farm was to go and collect the eggs, but to get to the henhouse you had to go through the stable. Jack would see me coming. Jack would wait until I got halfway past and then he would start to lean on me and there I was trying to push him off and him grinning from ear to ear. I got the eggs—that was fine.

And of course as the winter came and Jack was pressed into service with the old box sleigh with straw in the bottom and my Dad who was very God fearing had to go to church every Sunday. We all had to go to church. We used to go to Zion Church and behind the church there was a stable—I believe it was on Kent street—so when the farmers all got in to go to church they left their rigs there and the horses. When we came out, we all picked up our horses and off we trotted. Most of the time it worked very well, but sometimes it was very bad weather. That didn't matter—we still had to go to church; we had to sing in the choir and all that stuff which was a great thing anyway. Anyhow, this Sunday we all got back in the sleigh and it was storming quite badly and had been all during the service. Going in, we trotted along. Jack was really upset because he didn't want to be out in that weather. He made it very clear by prancing around when we were trying to

hitch him back up again. We were going along the North River Road. The plough had been on it. I don't know why they had gone out on Sunday—maybe they did go out. Anyway, the road had been ploughed and there were great big drifts and banks to either side of the road. Jack was happy because he was heading home. So he was prancing along nicely and we were sitting there enjoying the ride. As we got closer to the farm and Jack could smell the stable he picked up speed. Dad hung onto the reins trying to slow him down, but Jack took the bit between his teeth and he kept going. When he got to our driveway, of course there were great big banks where the snowplough had pushed the snow. Jack didn't stop. Jack didn't even slow down. Jack took a mighty leap over the snow bank and dumped us all out in the snow! It broke the shaft off the sleigh and Jack took off up the driveway dragging the sleigh behind him with the broken shaft. We picked ourselves up and dusted ourselves off. We had to tramp up the rest of the driveway. It was a long driveway. We got up to the house and there was Jack—standing by the stable door, ice still hanging on to the sleigh, and the broken shaft—with a big grin on his face—as much to say, "Gotcha!"

Barbara: Where was the farm?

Pat: On the North River Road. You know where the Garden Nursing Home is? That was our farm—both sides of the road. And the old house is still standing.

Hitching up the horse

Isabel: I was about fourteen. I was going to the store, and I told Mom I wasn't going to walk. I hitched up the sleigh. I got in and gave the horse a little push. She gave me a little nod and walked out of the sleigh. I had forgotten to hook up the traces!

Taking the reins

Donald: I remember going to church at Orwell Head, with my grandfather in the horse and wagon. He gave me the horse's reins for me to drive the horse. It made me feel pleased. My grandfather was a farmer.

Going for a horse & buggy ride

Tina: We were going to get grain from the shed. I was just five. The horse's name was Blaze because of a blaze on its forehead. The grain shed was about 1 ½ miles from home. It was a lot of fun and the passing cars did not bother the horse until a man that knew Dad was passing and blew his horn. Startled, Blaze jumped off the road. The reins were torn off, the buggy crashed, and we were thrown into the ditch. We weren't seriously hurt—just a few bumps and bruises, but it was painful. Blaze just loped on toward home and didn't stop until he got to the barn door. He had some cuts on his legs, but needed no stitches.

The man that caused the accident stopped his car, turned around, and helped us into his car, picking up broken buggy parts on the way. Getting home, Mother fixed our cuts while Dad and the man put Blaze into the barn and hooked a flat wagon behind the car. They went and got the buggy loaded on the wagon, brought it home, and stored it in the barn. It took a few weeks to get it fixed, and even longer to get Blaze comfortable in harness—first he was hitched to a small wagon but it was weeks before he settled down to pull the normal wagon.

Motor Vehicles

First vehicle

Richard: My story is about our first vehicle. My father had driven a car in his younger days. So anyway we had decided to buy a vehicle from Wendell Barber, in Charlottetown.

Tom: A car dealer?

Richard: A Dodge dealer—a landmark.

Ron: Somewhere on University.

Richard: So anyway we bought a '49 GMC half-ton [truck] and we had to get our neighbour drive us in to make the deal. The salesman had come out previous to that—I forget his name—can't remember my own name! [note, car salesmen made house calls!] Our neighbour had a license and he drove us in. He lived just down the road from us. We got all our business done, and we come home, and my father decided he would drive; he'd get behind the wheel after we dropped our neighbour off. He hadn't driven for 30 years, probably. So anyway, to make a long story short, he missed the gate, down into the ditch, and so on and so forth. We had to get the tractor down to get the car up through the field.

Pat: How embarrassing.

Richard: And the moral of the story is that he was driving the next morning.

Tom: So he got back on the horse, so to speak.

Old (British) cars

Pat: This is a story about how I learned to drive and the different cars that I drove. The story starts just a year after the war in 1945. I had recently returned from Canada as an evacuee and went back to London. My father was fighting of course in the war and he was demobbed. He was looking around for something to do to take up his time, and he got together with my uncle and decided that they were going to go into the used car business. Now after the war there was very little in the way of autos in England because nothing had been built during the war—it all went to Munitions and everything. Cars were at a premium. So they set about getting these old cars from auctions in various places, farmers fields, and stuff. They would drag them back to their garage and they would renovate them. My uncle was a mechanic of sorts and my Dad used to do the body work and clean out—what they basically did was tidy them up a bit and make sure they ran. In order to go and pick up these cars they needed extra drivers. I was only fifteen at the time but I was all gung-ho. I was an extra driver and I used to go along and come home with these amazing old cars. There were Bentleys and there was something called a Talbot which had a long hood—about six or seven feet long, probably more than that. When you sat behind the wheel you could barely see over the hood ornament. And then we had some all kinds of ancient Woolseys and we even had an old German squad car. Which I thought was really great—a 15 year old driving this German squad car. We got kind of known for our cars and people would come—not that we really did anything amazing, but of course people were anxious for a car no matter what kind it was.

Never a driver's license

Pat: After a few years I actually got a driver's license—but it wasn't a real driver's license—it was a learner's permit. At that point I decided I would move back to Canada, so I turned up here in Prince Edward Island and I went to the local drivers Bureau in Charlottetown and said, "I need a driver's license."

They said, "What have you got?"

And I produced my learner's permit from England.

"You've already got a license."

So I said, "Oh goody."

So they just handed me another one. So years have gone by and I'm now 85 and I've never had a proper license—just kept on renewing the old one. So that's my story about old cars.

Tom: How well do you drive do you think?

Pat: I'm an excellent driver—well heck I've been driving since I was 15 and I'm 85 now. No grave errors. Somebody once flew into the side of me and flew over my car and landed on the other side but that wasn't my problem.

Actually it is a real driver's license. Its just I never had a test, ever.

Tom: So the rules of the road are a mystery to you.

Pat: Yes, I just head the darn thing in the right direction and I know where the brake is and the accelerator and that's about it. Gone through a lot of cars. The moral of the story is don't come anywhere near me when I'm driving

Pat: What about you Tina? You have a license?

Tina: I drove for years without one. Being a farmer's daughter. That's driving a tractor mainly. But I [recently] gave it up.

Tom: For Lent?

Tina: For the rest of my life I'm afraid. Not that I wanted to but for myself I knew that I no choice. I didn't want to hurt anybody.

Pat: That never occurred to me.

Licenses for everyone

Tom: I don't have a whole lot of driving stories, but I do remember my father telling me when he was young in the late 1920s his father went to town and got driver's licenses for *everybody* in the family. I think he paid a dollar apiece and got a license. There was no test, there was no nothing, and my grandmother, to the best of my knowledge, never learned to drive but had a driver's license. I think the regulations have gotten so much stricter since then.

Road feel

Tom: I might stick in here a story much more recent. In my later years I had a friend who said that I ought to decide what I wanted to do with my life before I was drooling over the edge of a wheelchair, and that rather graphic thing led me to a sort of a bucket list. One of the things on my bucket list, which was very short, was a sports car, and I ended up finding a used Miata, a little Japanese 2-seater—that's a two point zero zero seater—no extra room at all. I had it for several years, but I eventually sold it because when we moved to PEI I discovered two things 1) Driving a top-down automobile when it's above 90 Fahrenheit and the sun is beating down is too hot, so you have to put the top up and turn the air conditioning on and when it's below about 60 Fahrenheit it's too cold with the wind whistling by, so it really looks stupid sitting there with a parka at 60 degrees riding along with your top down. The second thing was back when it first came out they advertised how it gave you 'road feel'—in touch with your environment kind of thing, When we got to PEI we discovered that the last thing you want to feel on PEI is the patches on the roads—the patches on the patches—so we kept it a very short time. It was nice, but sailing is better, actually.

Antique trucks

Barbara: You have a fantastic story about Pres MacIntyre's truck. He can tell you: It belonged to Dr. Pres. MacIntyre.

Richard: Dr. Pres MacIntyre: He was what you call a Doctor back then.... And this truck was out behind. He had race horses, and he bought this truck—new. It was a one-ton back then...

Tom: Any idea about when—what time...

Richard: 1954 They put a low rack on it, which they took off and put this—they had a big high box for hauling horses, and I made the mistake of not getting a picture of it.

So anyway When I bought it, didn't buy it from him—I bought it from a guy that worked for him, and I used to see it out behind when I'd take my Father to the Dr. Id never known I'd ever own it. Anyway, I saw it advertised in the

paper so down I went and I bought it. It had the high box with (Royal Sanders) marked on the side in Roman Letters. (His brother was an artist.) It was on a half-circle. The writing was in a half-circle with a horse's head in the centre. I'm so mad that I didn't get a picture of it. I had no use for the big box, so I took it off and I made a smaller one out of it.

Tom: OK and lost the...

Richard: and I tried to get a picture from the Family—but the Family were all gone. There was a picture in the Office—'cause I used to see it when I'd be waiting.

I still have the Manual. The Manual was in the Dash with his name where he signed for the whole business.

Tom: What brand of truck was it?

Richard: Dodge

Tom: Dodge truck. OK. I know a guy who loves Chevys and hates Fords.

Richard: Right now there's around 15 thousand miles on it—38 thousand kilometres [math?].

Tom: So you're still using it?

Richard: I used it on the Farm.

Tom: You still own it though.

Richard: Oh yeah. When I stopped farming I restored it. It didn't need much restoring. The material in them old cabs—You hit the cab it'd be like hitting that table there. So anyway, the only thing I had to do was put a frame on it. We tried to fix it but it was rusted out. I was very, very lucky because a half-ton is the same. Everything was the same.

Tom: *Now* you mean?

Richard: Back then.

Tom: The same as...

Richard: Same (turns?) and everything—back axle and all that.

Tom: Oh, the half-ton and the ton were the same.

Richard: I got one for a hundred bucks.

Tom: Parts for a 50-something truck are...

Richard: The only thing that's not original on it is the gas tank. It's a homemade gas tank.

Tom: And they'll pass it?

Richard: Oh yeah. Them things—the only draw-back was no gauge You had to guess at how much gas was in it.

Another thing that I tried to get for it was parking lights. The parking lights all rusted around the rims—chrome rims. So there's a place in Toronto called Dodge City. So I phoned there—he says he have a list of names of people looking for them.

Tom: 'Cause they rusted out a lot, apparently.

Richard: [indistinct] Some switched over. I never liked...

Tom: Then everything's different?

Richard: It's the original motor—flat-head motor.

Tom: Um hm... a six.

Richard: Flat six 90 horsepower [indistinct] this big high box and 3 horses. It would be so slow. You'd think you were flying at 30 [m.p.h.].

Tom: So how many gears? Was it 3-speed?

Richard: 3 speed.

Tom: So the differential must have been geared very low.

Richard: [indistinct] try it in a field in low gear [indistinct] and reverse was slow too.

Tom: It wouldn't be very useful on the Interstate.

Richard: You'd be a long time getting anywhere—but I don't mind that. I had it up west one time.

Tom: You mean west on the Island?

Richard: Yeah. I got a load of railway ties. We had a long trip. You want to drop in sometime and take a look at her.

Tom: Do you have pictures?

Richard: Oh, I have lots of pictures.

A new Model T

Tina: A little tiny story. This had somethin' to do with the antique cars [that Richard talked about earlier]. It was a Model T Ford. At that time it was a new one.

Tom: A new Model T.

Tina: My Dad would come home from work. I was 7 years old. (I can still date myself, that's beside the point. I don't think there's too many younger than me here anyways) My father came home, he was doing good—it was a dirt road and he'd sink in this deep [gesture of depth] into the mud but he came home. It was a churchyard that we were living on. There was one driveway on the left and one driveway on the right. My Dad came home and he got the car slowed down and he drove in and got it parked in front of the house. He wanted to take everybody for a ride. So we all got ready and got in the car as we were—none of us were really dirty—my baby brothers were clean, my baby sister was clean—she was the baby at the time—and we all got in the car and my father got the car turned around and he was going to go out by the same gate that he had gone in.

We told him, "Dad, you'd better turn a little bit more to the left. Turn a little bit more left."

He was busy. He was driving. He had her floored—right into the gatepost! That's as far as we got for our ride. So we had to push the car off the gatepost, bring it back to the house, and get everybody out back out. Mom went and finished her supper and the three older ones—well I was only seven—and my two older brothers fixed the post; put in a new one. The post had broken right off and it was a 10" by 10" post. It had broken right in two, so he had had her floored. Even though he wasn't going very fast to start with, he really rammed her. I was mad was because I ending up having to help take out the pieces that were broken from underneath. I wasn't impressed. But we had a ride. I can say I drove in a model T—a new one.

Tom: Was it damaged?

Tina: Not really. There was a solid steel bumper on the front of it. It didn't even have a scratch mark on it. I guess the post was made of a sort of a soft wood and it had its own gate it had to be closed in the evening—all the gates were closed at that place. That was my first ride with a car—in a car but not driving.

Tom: I assume they hadn't invented seat belts back then. And airbags. But nobody got hurt.

Tina: No. Nobody was hurt.

Cat Under the Hood

Helen: On a cold winter day, I was at one of the many funerals which I attend. It was in Wellspring Presbyterian Church I Peter's Road; and I came home from the funeral and went into my apartment for a short time. I came out of my apartment and started up my car and drove to Georgetown to Mass at St. James Roman Catholic Church. Mass began at 4:00 p.m. When I came out of church after Mass a few of the people who had attended mass, came to me and said there was a cat crying under the hood of my car. I said "Wow! How could that be?" I lifted the hood and sure enough all I could see were two big eyes and a faint 'meow'. I asked one of the kind people to take out the battery from my car, and to my fear, the cat was caught under the fly wheel!

I called a gentleman who had done work on my car to come and veterinarian in Montague and told him about a cat who was badly hurt and to have someone at the animal hospital when I arrived in Montague! The gentleman took the cat to the animal hospital and the vet took x-rays and found that the cat had a broken spine and two broken legs, and it was better that I have the cat 'put to sleep'.

By this time I was really upset and I said "no, some child might own the cat and I don't want to put the cat to sleep when it did not belong to me. The vet told me that it would cost me a great deal of money and the cat might never be right, and that he was an out-door male cat--a stray. While I was making up my mind the vet had to give the cat a needle for pain. After much persuasion on the part of the veterinarian I said: "OK" to put the cat to sleep.

The next day I Montague I saw a picture of the cat on a bulletin board with a telephone number to call concerning the cat. Right away, by looking at the 'cat's eyes" I knew it was the same cat that was caught in my car. I came home and called the lady whose telephone no was on the bulletin board. I told the lady the story about the cat that was caught in my car and that I took the cat to the vet and they had to put the cat to sleep. The lady insisted that her cat was a family cat—a female cat—who had escaped when the family were moving into a house I Montague. Well, at least I tried.

The next day I had to have my car put back together—on a cold day that was quite a process—then to make matters worse, one head light on my car was out. I went to pick up a couple in the trailer park in Montague and the police trailed me to the park, and told me about my car light being out and I had to have it fixed. Well, the man that I picked up said maybe the light would come on if I got out and kicked the car. Bingo on comes the light. The police said "not good enough, you will have to get the light fixed" which I did the next day. I went to the police station to show them the paperwork and payment and that was all okay.

The police told me I the winter before I start the car, always tap lightly on the hood and if an animal is under the hood they will flee. Animals always go under the hood for warmth.

Ferries

Georgetown ferry

Tom: We're just recording memories about the ferry across to Georgetown.

Corena: [pointing to the picture] That was called the Montague 2, and ran between lower Montague and Georgetown. I was born close to where the

ferry used to come in. There was a wharf in lower Montague, naturally, and I lived just up from the ferry. In fact, when I was born, I was born at home, and the doctor, Dr. Kennedy, came over on the ferry boat from Georgetown. I was born in May. He came over on the ferry boat. In fact his home is still a beautiful home right on the Main Street—the corner of the Main Street and Water Street, I guess. It is in Georgetown—a beautiful older home there.

Tom: Was Georgetown the big city then?

Corena: Oh yes. What I remember specifically 'bout Georgetown, I loved to go over on the ferry. In fact my Dad's brother at one time, Uncle Philip, worked on that Ferry. In Georgetown there was an ice cream parlour, Fougere's ice cream parlour. I remember that well because, growing up we had Poole's Store in Lower Montague, but you couldn't get ice cream there—not in those years. Anyway that was a big treat to go over on the ferry and go to Fougere's for ice cream. I remember it well.

Train crossing on the ferry

[part of conversation about Royal Winter Fair train trip]

Tom: Did the boxcar start from the Island?

Ron: Yes.

Tom: And that was back when the ferry…

Ron: Right, right onto the boat.

Tom: What was it like?

Ron: We left from Kensington, PEI.

Tom: And you got to the ferry—did they put the engine on too, or just the car?

Ron: I can't remember all the details. They shunt you back in there.

Tom: Did the locomotive cross over too, or did they just put the cars on?

Ron: Yeah.

Tom: So there's the locomotive on the other side ready to go. I'd heard such stories in Anne of Green Gables. Some of [LM Montgomery's] stories talk about the passenger train being taken right across.

Pat: Oh yeah I can remember back that far.

TRAINS

Walking was faster

Miriam: We went to Grandview station to go to Charlottetown.

Richard: I never did make a trip to Charlottetown on the train.

Miriam: We did.

Barbara: Well my husband enlisted in the Air Force and he had to go up to Summerside to enlist so they got a free train ride up to Summerside and back again. It took them four hours to get from Charlottetown to Summerside so on the way back they decided to walk and they got to Charlottetown before the train did. It stopped at everybody's back gate and picked up the cream and everywhere along the road. They were slow.

Miriam: Well, they used to have babies on the train going to town.

Barbara: When they stopped at every cattle crossing.

Backing up

Tom: Talk about the train, since the conversation has wandered off there. It took a long time?

Miriam: We used to meet the train in Grandview and my sister was a deaf mute. And she and I went up to meet our father one evening and the train stopped and Robert MacPhee got off and there was no father there. So the train went on up the track, but it didn't go up very far before it backed up. So he got off.

Tom: He missed it?

Miriam: No, they were drinkin'!

Barbara: Had he been in the town working or something?

Miriam: No, no. He was just in for the day and he used to do a lot of business

with potatoes and turnips and whatever. Robert MacPhee was his trucker.

Tom: This a relative of Roger MacPhee

Miriam: No, no [general laughter in background] And the train used to go to Vernon and it would make the loop in Vernon and when it came into Montague here, it went around the turntable with nowhere else to go, so it would just go back out to Murray Harbour.

Tom: Do you know the pit of the turntable is still there?

Miriam: Yeah.

Tom: So it came into Montague coming up the river?

Miriam: No. It didn't come up the river. It came up from Vernon River—it came in through Annandale, didn't it?

Richard: That was the Georgetown train. You're talking about the Murray Harbour train. The Murray Harbour train came through Vernon River.

Tom: So what came into Montague?

Barbara: The Montague/Georgetown train. It came from Charlottetown down

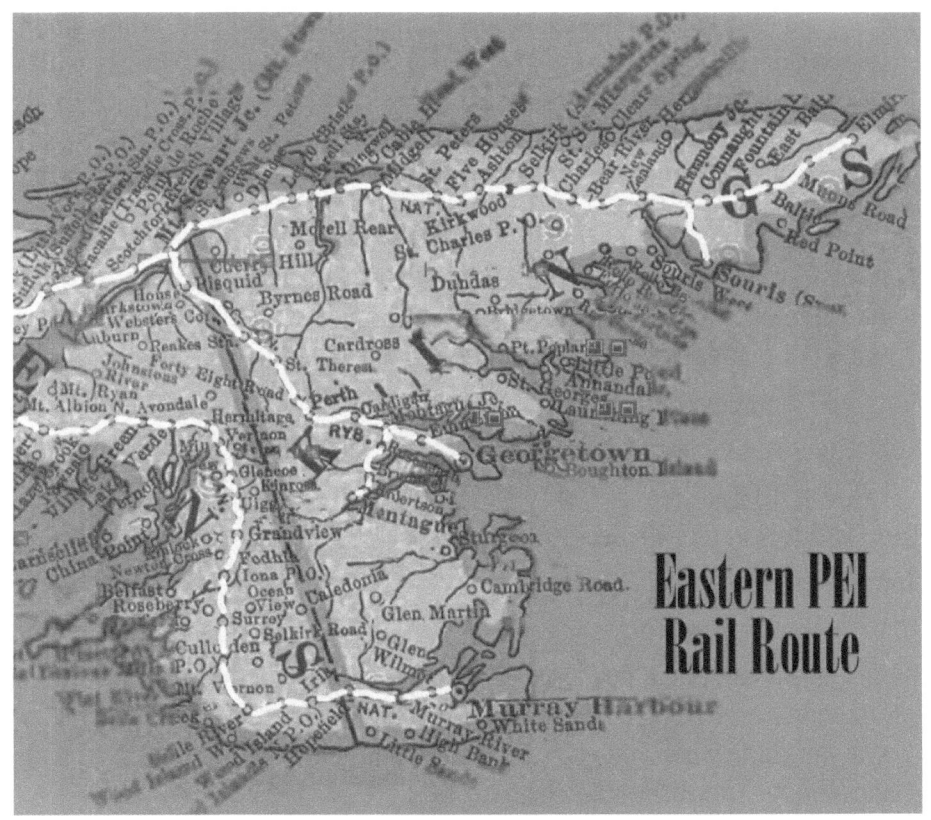

around Mt. Stewart didn't it, Richard? It came into Montague and then down to Georgetown. It came through Cardigan too.

Miriam: Yeah, there was a station in Cardigan, a station in Georgetown, and a station in Montague.

Barbara: At night you could hear the train all the way down the river you could hear it all the way across at my place when it was getting into Georgetown in the evening

Tom: What I mean is, the tracks ended at Montague, didn't they?

[at this point discussion collapsed into a debate about the route(s) of the rail lines].

Near miss

dd: Before Brudenell School amalgamated with Montague we had a Volkswagen car. I used to drive the children to school. One morning I dropped them off, and that day the roads were icy. Coming home I had to cross the railroad and the car stopped on the track with the train coming. I stepped on the gas and just managed to get off the track. The conductor asked me if I was all right. "I am now," I said.

Trip to Toronto

Ron: At 13 years old I went to the Royal Winter Fair in a boxcar, looking after the cattle on the way up, milking them and feeding them. Over the cattle we had a loft made where we slept and done our cooking.

Tom: And where was this fair?

Ron: The Royal Winter Fair in Toronto. So we went from here to Toronto in the box car—a three-day journey back then.

Tom: Was this in the winter?

Ron: November.

Tom: So it was pretty cool.

Ron: Well it wasn't that, because you had cattle that kept the car warm. I don't remember ever being cold—you were up there. You stayed right in the barn with the cattle when you got [to the fair] and looked after them. You had to show them. They had to be clean.

Pat: Did you sell the cattle while you were there?

Ron: No, I was working for a farmer. No, his bull was Grand Champion that year.

Pat: Just showing the cattle.

Ron: Stanley Hurry out of Winsloe—actually I worked on his farm when I was a child. And went to the Royal Winter Fair with him.

Ron: An interesting trip.

Tom: What was Toronto like?

Ron: Well I had an older sister up there. She picked me up and took me to a hockey game in Toronto. It was quite an eye-opener for me.

Tom: You were 13, so that was definitely the big city.

Ron: Yes.

Riding among soldiers

Tina: The only thing I can say is I came from Winnipeg to Ottawa in a train car. They had forgotten about my feet [disability]. My car was loaded with the military coming back from overseas.

Pat: Those sailors!

Tina: Soldiers, sailors, airmen the whole thing.

Pat: And how old were you?

Tina: I was 14. I had whistles when I came in the door I went straight through to the other end and I was still whistled at. The conductor said, "You're in *that* car." I looked at him and I said, "Where am I supposed to sit? On somebody's lap?"

Pat: You were still a virgin at the end of this trip?

Tina: Oh yes! There was one fellow, I'd say he was about 20, he came and put his arm around me and says, "You can have my seat." So I sat down in his seat. The guy beside me—I wasn't too sure about him, but he was very gentlemanly. He was older. He was like a father to me for that trip. And the guy whose seat I was in, he went and pushed a couple of the guys over and he sat on the edge there right next door to me, across the hall, and he was watchin'. One of the guys got up and looked at me and he just went like this [gesture not recorded]. I guess he must have been somebody extra special in the group that he was with, when he went like this, that guy sat down. He turned white as a sheet; he wasn't moving. Nobody else moved after that. They came home to Ottawa the same as when I had gotten on.

Tom: You might put it in words that you made a gesture side-to-side and a head-shaking both saying, "No thank you."

ADVERTISING SLOGANS

Tiger in the tank

Tom: Yeah okay, we'll digress a little bit and talk about the tails that hung out of the gas tank—the Tiger In The Tank—which we discussed only it wasn't being recorded. You don't remember them?

Barbara: Oh yes, I remember them well. It was a commercial for ESSO—put a tiger in your tank. I think that became Tony the Tiger. Eventually there was this tail—not a real tail but it was striped like a tiger's and it would hang over the back of the car because the gas tank filler used to be located at the centre about where the license plate usually went. You could hook this 'Tiger Tail' with elastic around the gas tank filler-pipe. It was the craze and people went around with a tiger in their tank.

UTILITIES

HOUSES

Moving by horses

Ethel: My mother and father were married in 1929. Dad had property, so they bought a 2-story house which had to be hauled to their land [about ¼ mile away]. Skids were put under the house and it was hauled by horses and put over a hole in the ground which would be dug out by shovel later so as to have a bigger cellar.

Building from scratch

Ruth: In 1875 my grandfather, Duncan Campbell, built a house for his new bride, Margaret MacLeod. For the first two years they lived in the first floor, adding a second floor as they could. By 1885, with 3 children, they had completed the second floor for use.

In the early 1920s, my Dad started to build our own house on the farm. He cut the lumber in our own woodlot and had it sawed and cut as he wanted, including hardwood for the flooring, which he had kiln-dried. The cement foundation was done—26 x 28'—and closed in for the winter months. In April 1922 my grandfather, a first-rate carpenter of the times, took over the job of building the home for us. He knew how to cut the lumber so there were no mistakes—all sawing done by the rip saw—no electric saws or easy cutting in those days. That summer work really progressed: the framing was done, the roof was done, and the enclosure was ready. The flue was built in the centre of the house. The downstairs had a paneled kitchen, pantry, dining room and living room with an open stairwell in the living room. The second floor was laid out with four single bedrooms and what became a bathroom—in early days served as a bedroom. It is very much the same today, some 70 years later. During the busy summer days Dad had help from some neighbours, and November 20, 1922 was moving day. It was a cold day to be moving. In the morning the stove was moved from the old house and the fire started. The new house had a hidden woodbox under the stairs, which is still there. By noon we had lunch in the new house.

In the afternoon an elderly neighbour, Jim Ross, called by. He said he could not spend another year by himself as his health was not so well and he would like to have a cup of tea in the new home. My grandmother gave him some home-made biscuits and jam and a hot cup of tea while the younger folks were busy moving. After thanking my grandmother, he said goodbye, and made his way to his old home where a week later he was admitted into what at that time they called the 'poor house' That was the last time I recall seeing him, and I heard of his passing away a year later. His farm changed hands and has been sold quite a few times since and the house and barn were torn down and burned so that makes another passing era.

HEATING

Winterizing

Ruth: When the fall came they went to the wood lot to cut wood for winter heat. Oil was not even an option back then. Many times I heard my elders speak of getting up in the morning to find the kettle frozen hard to the stove. There was no insulation—the houses were just boarded up the studding and then shingled on the outside. This only slowed the North wind. If it was available, many rooms were papered with newspaper to stop some of the drafts that were coming in at the corners. When wallpaper became available they thought it was a God-send as it was thick and heavy.

I've been told the early settlers always banked their houses up to the windowsills with clay to keep the frost out. They liked to see lots of snow as it made the building that much warmer over the winter.

Out in the snow

Mary Ellen: There were three wood stoves to keep the house warm and many times we had to go out on a snow bank in our pajamas and coat because of a flue fire. It was scary.

ELECTRICITY

Arrival of Electricity

Tom: Anybody remember before electricity?

Richard: I spent 40% of my life without electricity. We were without electricity until I was about 17, I guess, or more. It was quite a change for the house to light up and to have a radio you wouldn't have to be buying batteries for. And then we switched our water system from a gas engine to an electric engine—same pump and everything, just changed the pulleys. We got it done in the middle of winter. My father was sick in bed and I was only 17 and they were asking me—I was supposedly the boss at that age. It was in the winter, in January that they put the line in.

Barbara: So they asked you where to put the outlets?

Richard: There were different questions they was asking me 'cause my father was laid up in bed.

Barbara: Did you have to tell them where to put the switches?

Richard I don't know it was switches but they were asking me some questions I don't remember exactly what they were.

Tom: Had there been other houses nearby? Did electric hook-ups sort of spread?

Richard I can't remember if the neighbours had it before us or not. I imagine they did. We were usually in the hind quarter.

Barbara: I was just going to say, on the topic of getting the electricity in, that on our farm my father built a windmill. We had wind power for quite a few years before the electricity came across. It [pumped water and] supplied the house and it supplied the barn. It supplied the water tanks for the cattle and I think about the same amount of water for the house and nothing else. [We had] kerosene lamps—we didn't have the Aladdin lamps. But then my mother was expecting me. It just so happened that Robert Clements had a cottage in lower Montague, and he ran Montague Electric at the time, so he ran wires—Georgetown had been wired because it was a town—he ran a line across the harbour to his cottage, and my father had him hook us up to electricity. My mother was very pleased that we had the electricity by the time I was born. We had minimal lighting, like Pat said [in the next piece], upstairs. It was just the bulb hanging from the ceiling, but downstairs it was enough to run a hot-plate in the summer when it got really warm and supply the downstairs with electricity, but we still retained the windmill. He kept that for the cattle and pumping water into the barn and it was quite a large windmill. I think the only reason we finally took it down was because I insisted on climbing it at a very early age and Mom was always scared that I was going to fall and break something, if not my neck. So eventually he took the windmill down, but that was in 1945 that we got the electricity and we had the first electric radio on the road. I think it would be about 1951 or '52 that he took the windmill down.

Pat: Interesting. When you say they ran a line across the Harbour, was it under the water?

Barbara: A cable. Yes. Under the water—he was very advanced for his time.

Tom: He didn't worry about anchors?

Barbara: Oh no, that wouldn't have happened. I don't know how he did it. Nellie might be able to tell you or she might not. It might not have mattered to a young girl. Yeah, we ran the cable across into his cottage and up the road to us. But there were at one time in the '50s or '60s three windmills left on the Island in King's County, but they're all gone now.

Shock in the tub

Tom: Do you remember when you got electricity?

Pat: No, that was before my days. I arrived in Canada in 1940, and the house was old, but it had been wired. Very rudimentary—upstairs all the lights hung from the middle of the ceiling. You had to run into your bedroom in the dark and feel around for the chain to put the light on.

Tom: There weren't any wall switches?

Pat: No, not upstairs. I think we had wall switches downstairs but bedrooms were considered, you know, just sort of an offshoot. But we also had one in the bathroom that hung over the bathtub, so you had to make sure you put the light on or off *before* you got into the tub. My sister and I had a bath one afternoon—we were going somewhere in the evening. Our mother ran the tub and we got in the tub. It was raining at the time so it was quite dark and the light was on.

We were sitting there splashing and having a good time and my sister said, "Oh, the sun has just come out," so she stood up and she grabbed the chain and there was an immediate screech. She flopped down again—a shock, of course. We tried it again, the same thing. [laughter]

Pat: Nobody told us. We were 9 and 11, you know. That was our first sort of shock.

Tom: So only by the grace of God are you here!

Pat: Yes, exactly, but I seem to think the electricity in those days wasn't as powerful as it is today?

[unidentified chorus]: No, probably 50 or 70 amps going through the line.

Tom: Enough amps to kill you. [It is the voltage rather than the current capability of a circuit that leads to electrocution—a few thousandths of one amp is all that it takes!]

Pat: We didn't even realize even then until we mentioned it to our mother and she said, "Oh I forgot to tell you not to pull the chain while you're in the tub."

Tom: The electrician in me is totally dismayed!

Plumbing: in and out

Wells

Richard: For instance, consider our water supply. Our first source of water at home was a well in the yard built of stone in a three-foot circle, and thirty to forty feet deep. How they were dug is a mystery to me, but when it was finished, there was a windlass with a crank, a rope, and a bucket. The bucket was lowered into the well until it hit the water; then, when full, it was cranked up to the surface. The well usually had a wooden cover on it to keep small animals from falling in and polluting the water.

After that well, we dug our first well to use a hand pump at the porch. A pipe was run through the wall to water the cattle in a large tub outside. That way they had to come over to the house once a day for water and back to the stalls again to be tied up.

A later change was to jack the house up and dig a basement under the porch. At that time we installed a jet pump in the old well, run by a gas engine. The outside tub was still used to water the cattle.

Electricity came to the farm in the mid-fifties so we then changed the pump motor and dug a water line to the barn and installed drinking bowls for the cattle.

I believe that the most changes to agriculture happened in my generation.

Outhouse blew over

Mary Ellen: We had an outhouse, and many times it blew over.

Outhouse burned down

Winnie: We had an outhouse at home. It was not a comfort station, but it was serviceable, and Dad put lime in it to keep down the flies in the summer and the stench, and my mother had passed away and Auntie was looking after us. It was a full-time job—there were seven of us and we were not the most obedient children that were around. Of course I had my nose in a book, but my little brother disappeared for a while, and suddenly somebody said, "The outhouse is on fire."

Well we looked and sure enough, it was on fire and a car stopped on the side of the road and this gentleman came in and my aunt and I were trying to pump water into a wash tub to go and empty it on top of this thing, and we wouldn't have been able to carry it and it wouldn't have been much use when we did get there. She sent one of the older children down to the next farm where Dad was working with my grandfather, and they came back, and they just knocked the thing down and let it burn. That was the end of the outhouse!

Tom: So did they have to build another one?

Winnie: I don't think they did, actually. I think they partitioned off a part in the barn that served as an outhouse, because by that time we didn't have any animals anymore so they just made a little kind of a room in there.

Tom: But you didn't have indoor plumbing?

Winnie: No, God no!

Indoor plumbing

Corena: I did [have indoor plumbing], my whole life.

Winnie: Lucky you!

Corena: Where we lived, which, you know, was five miles out of Montague—people from the States had owned the home before my parents, and there was a bathroom, but we also had an outhouse. That outhouse had been there.

I remember what my brother did one time. Like Mom would—in the summertime, say, she would use that [outhouse] sometimes rather than troop all through the house—she had to go through the kitchen, the hall to go upstairs 'cuz that's where the bathroom was. But this one time my grandmother was outside and used it. My brother locked her in. [laughter] I remember being so cross at him—so cross that he did that—because my grandmother lived with us and I was very fond of her. He turned the knob, you know, and there was poor Nana out in the outhouse calling.

Winnie: Brothers and sisters played on each other a lot in the washroom.

Corena: Oh, yes.

Winnie: Or at Halloween time, upsetting it. That was a great trick the young people thought that was great to upset the outhouse.

Outhouse at school

Corena: The outhouse at the school, I felt was the coldest place on Earth, for sure. You had to leave the school, go down, and on one side it was for the girls, and the other side for the boys. And the boys tried to bore holes through the wall to our side—I remember that—there was talk about that. But that had to be, in my experience, *the* coldest place. For sure, there weren't too many comforts.

Water heater problems

Pat: About the old house: when we first moved in there was a lot to do, and we spent most of our waking hours doing repairs. We were only there a couple of days and the pump wasn't working so I asked our neighbour—I didn't have a phone at the time—if she knew of a plumber and she said, "Oh yes, I know the plumber." So she gave me the plumber's name and I went and got in touch with this plumber and he said, "Oh sure, I'll be there tomorrow." which of course could mean anything. Surprise, surprise, he turned up the next day more out of curiosity to see the odd people that had bought this old haunted house. That was fine. He came in with his helper—a man about 70 years old. Anyway he tried to crank the pump over and it wasn't going. It would crank for a while and then it would stop. So he said to his helper, "Now you go down cellar and see what's happening down there."

And the helper said, "What me? I couldn't go down in the cellar. This place is haunted." And he was really quite upset.

I said, "I'll go down with you and hold your hand, okay?"

So he very reluctantly followed me down the cellar and finally got whatever he had to do, came back up and flipped the switch. That was fine—we got water. So off they went, and I continued with my wallpapering.

When my son came home from school and he said, "Mom the house is on fire."

I said, "Oh it can't be on fire."

So I got off my ladder, flying down stairs—sure enough the kitchen was full of steam, I mean absolutely full.

I'm standing there thinking, "[Darn] another emergency. What'll I do this time. There's something going on down there." So I got down on my knees and I looked and there was a shutoff valve right by the door. So I thought I'll do something with this, so I shut the valve off and the steam gradually subsided and everything sort of was visible again.

I thought, "I wonder what happened here." Then I stood and looked at the tank. On the tank there was a sign that said, "DO NOT TURN ON THE ELECTRICITY UNTIL THE TANK IS FILLED WITH WATER" and of course the plumber hadn't read that, so of course when the water started coming in he thought, "There you go lady, you're all set," and toddled off. So it had filled up to a certain level and then of course overheated and that's where we got the steam.

Tom: Burned out the element probably.

Pat: No, actually I got to it in time.

That evening I was invited to join the women's Institute which was meeting a couple of days after that. Somebody came, "Oh you'll have to join our Institute." I said, Oh good, I'd love that."

During the afternoon my oldest son said, "It's a good day to launch the boat today because the tide is high."

So I said, "Okay."

We didn't have anything to launch it with; we were going to have to push it. We didn't have a trailer under the boat. I should mention at this point, it wasn't a *very* big boat. It was just something he was going to use for his mussel business.

So he said, "All hands to push the boat." At that point I just got the stove going, getting dinner.

"Okay," he said, "You have to come and help us push the boat."

They got rollers under the boat—probably tree trunks or something—and my job was to, when they pushed the boat, pick up the rollers, run around, and put them back in front of the boat. This continued down the driveway— we were doing really well—she was rolling along nicely until I slipped on the wet grass and the boat went over the top of me and I was trapped underneath it by my legs. They're laughing because it was funny and I'm saying, "Help, help." One of them said, "Stop the boat, I think Mom is trapped underneath." Anyway they rescued me from under the boat and we got rolling again and she took off down the driveway like a bugger and over the guardrail and into the water with a big splash. So there we go, we got the boat launched.

I look back at the house and there was smoke pouring out of the chimney.

"Oh my gosh, I set fire to the chimney!" I hastened back up to the house and sure enough, the stove pipe was red hot going into the wall, and all I could do was stand there and watch it, hoping it didn't collapse. I shut all the dampers and eventually it cooled off and I was able to get dinner.

So that evening my friend came to pick me up to go to the Institute meeting and I met all these new people and my friend said, "What did you do today?" I said, "Well, I got run over by a boat and I set fire to the chimney."

Everybody thought I was a weird person. After that they were quite sure that I was weird.

TELEPHONES

In the early days

Richard: In early days we didn't have a phone. There was a service station on the road, Callahan's right on the corner there in Albury Plains. We used to go there to use the phone. Then one of the neighbours got the first phone and we used to sponge off them and use their phone. Of course you would have to wait your turn because there would usually be somebody on the line.

My uncle told me last week he never had a phone, and never had electricity. When he went to use the phone, he had no patience with all the women on the line talking with one another, baby making, cakes baking, cake making—whatever. "Put your cake in the oven. I have to use the phone!" he said.

Party lines

Veda: I lived in Winsloe and the telephone line from Charlottetown only came part way up our road —maybe a quarter of a mile from our place. In order for us to get the telephone we had to hook on the Covehead line, so my father wasn't in any rush in doing that because most of the calls he wanted to make were to Charlottetown. So for years we didn't have a telephone. If we needed to telephone we went to neighbours that did have a phone, but eventually I guess when dial telephone came, they allowed us to hook on to Charlottetown, so from that point on we had a telephone.

And of course people listened on the line. My grandmother was one of the worst ones for listening. One time we were visiting my parents after we were married and we had a little fella I guess he was about two then and of course he got at the phone and I picked it up from him and put it to my ear and this woman was saying, "What's that kid doing on the telephone— where's his parents?"

Barbara: How many were on your line?

Veda: My goodness, now that's more than I can tell you. Yeah, it would be several but I don't remember. Actually, I didn't live at home when it was put in. Now that I think about it, that was after I was married. I don't think it was until later we had the telephone.

Barbara: Was it the box on the wall or did you have one that sat on the desk?

Veda: I think it sat on the table.

Barbara: Probably on the wall?

Veda: No, not on the wall. I know Kent was able to get at it. I think it was on the table.

Barbara: Well, the first one that we had was a box on the wall and when you wanted to ring you rang the number in.

[?]: How many rings?

Barbara: One of them was two long and a short but I'll leave that. It took forever....

Richard: Everybody had a 2-long or one long and one short and so on and so forth. There was about ten on the line in some areas and soon as you picked up you'd hear the clicks all along the line

Barbara: They'd hear the rings.

Richard: They'd be listening in.

Barbara: And if you picked it up and all the clicks came in, the more people picked up the less you could hear. So eventually, the person calling couldn't make the call.

Waiting for the line

Miriam Nicholson: When did I get my phone first phone? Probably in '48 or '47.

Barbara: You were way ahead of us.

Miriam: Yeah. I remember the people putting in the phone lines and the power about the same time and you used to go and get the phone and you might wait half an hour for it. And there was always somebody listening.

Tom: You had to jump in?

Miriam: You kept waitin' and waitin' and finally—the teenagers liked to stay on and finally you'd say, "Can I have the line for a minute please?" so you might get it and you might not.

Tom: Were there good and bad people on the line?

Miriam: Oh yeah! Let's just say tenish, twelve probably—

Richard: The most important thing, how did you phone up a date?

Miriam: I didn't phone for dates.

Richard: Everybody knew you.

Miriam: That's your problem. I never had that problem. They never phoned for dates. You had to go out and look for them.

Party line (dis)courtesy

Tina: We had just gotten a telephone—there had been no telephone where we were living in Ontario, southeast of Ottawa. The line was a party line. As it turned out, five other people jumped on as well. We had been living there for several months. I had married. Even though my daughter, Barbara, was just a little 2 year old, she knew her name, her phone number, and her address—the whole thing. This one day I was quite sick and was trying to get ahold of my sister-in-law to take me to the doctor (she lived about 5 miles away).

She tried to call for me but there was somebody already on the phone. "Mommy needs help! Mommy needs help! This is Barbara. Mommy needs help!" (The neighbours all knew who Barbara was. She was an adopted child so everybody knew, but she was new then.)

Somebody said, "Get off of the phone! Children are not supposed to be on the phone." I could hear this, but I couldn't get through to them.

So Barbara came over to me and said, "Mommy they don't let me talk on the phone."

It took quite a bit of my strength but I got to the phone and got through to them, "I need a doctor and ambulance and I need my sister-in-law to help me get ready for the ambulance (it was about as far as from Montague to Charlottetown to the ambulance). Finally I heard *click, click, click* and I realized everybody was off. I told her what number to call.

Jean, my sister-in-law, answered and she told her, "Mommy needs help." Next thing the phone went dead at the other end—that was all she needed. Next thing I knew her car was coming into the yard. That's one of my first telephone experiences.

Operators

Richard: In our previous discussion of phones and party lines I forgot to mention one of the most important things—the operator. I guess there were two shifts.

[unrecognizable comment here]

Richard: So did they stay on 24 hours a day?

Barbara: 'Till 10.

Richard: So if you wanted to phone after 10 o'clock, you wouldn't get through, was it?

Barbara: When you rang, a little button came down and [the operator] would get up and connect you.

Richard: So that was 24 hours. So that was one of the most important aspect of the phone.

Operators I've known

Barbara: I remember one operator well. This recollection is when I lived on the farm and we had a box phone on the wall—the very first one we got. You could call people on your line just by the number of rings you put in. If you wanted someone on *another* line you had to go 'long distance' through the operator. To reach her you had to press a little button on the phone box and then ring the operator. The operator was in Montague. Pearl's Phone board was in Montague and sometimes she was a little bit cranky. So anyway you push the button and you ring and if you rang and she didn't answer you'd get a little impatient so you'd push the button and ring ring ring ring ring ring ring ring ring and say, "Come on." Then she'd come on, "Don't be ringing so hard. You're ringing my ears off." If you're lucky she'd ask you for the number. She had to ring from her switchboard to get someone in Georgetown or anywhere else, but if she had a bad day she could give you an awful going over.

When I worked, it was for fun—not for pay. I worked at the telephone office in Georgetown along with Mrs. Easton. I was friends with her daughter. She had a shift that she had to take both girls, so the board was all set up. It was a huge board. We had all these plugs—Concords was the word—sitting in holes in front of you like a dashboard. When someone wanted you to make a connection, all the numbers had little brass plates with a plug in them and when they wanted to connect, that cover would fall down and it would buzz, and you would plug in *that* cord. You would talk to the person on the other line and find out who they wanted, and then you had to plug into that person. It got really busy at times. That's how it worked. At night we took turns. I would sleep on the couch that was put there for that reason and once in awhile the phone would ring. It would wake us up—no problem there—and you could turn that off.

"No Its *My* Baby"

Pat: My first experience with party line telephones was when we moved up to Summerside. It would have been about 1954, and we moved to an area called St. Eleanor's, and there was a road called Linkletter Road and everybody on the road was a Linkletter unless they were a Clark. Anyway, there was 21 people on the road and we were number 21 getting hooked up. The old fellow next door to us—his name was Clark—ran a farm and was the person who climbed up the pole and hooked you on when he wasn't milking cows and stuff. This was a really rural area.

Anyway, one winter my sister who lived in Charlottetown was expecting a baby and so we went to Charlottetown and picked up her two older children and that would be the first of January. She was expecting around then. The weather was getting bad so we thought we'd go early and pick up the babies which were three and four. We came back and all of us in the truck. I had two of my own. We got settled in. I had all these little kids who were driving me nuts. We waited patiently for the babies to come. There was another neighbour along the road who was waiting for a baby too—her daughter's baby—and about the same. So every time the phone rang, she would rush and pick it up, and I would rush and pick it up, and everybody else along the road would rush and pick it up. The time went on and it got longer and longer. I was trying to get babies out to play in the snow—they should go out.

Four of them get dressed up and three of them would say, "Its too cold." And one would refuse to go out at all and just sit. Time went by and one evening, quite late, the phone rang. I thought it was my line, so I picked up.

My neighbour picked up and she said, "No, no, Pat, it's not your baby, it's my baby."

And I said, "No its not," so we got into this argument.

Finally the person on the phone said, "M_o_o_o_m" and I thought, "[Darn] that's not my baby—that's her baby."

Ours finally arrived another two weeks later. I was climbing walls, but anyway that was my experience with the telephone.

Later Phones

Dora: We never had a phone or nothing like that.

Mary: [laughing] We had a party line.

Arlene: Everybody had a party line.

Dora: We had a party line out here when we first got our phone.

Arlene: Oh, yeah. When we moved here, we boarded next door and it was the old type. Doug couldn't get over the phones—it really got to him.

Mary: How old was he when you moved down?

Arlene: He was eight—up in Ontario, the phones were like they are today. He thought that was something else.

Dora: We had a party line first when we got out here, and I think we were one of the first to get a private phone.

FAMILY MEMORIES

Third of eight

Arlene: Now [Mary], tell us something about you.

[tea was poured and Doug brought in the bannock and sweets.]

Mary: I'm from the next generation, born in '54—the same generation as your children. I was born in Amherst, Nova Scotia. I'm the third in a family of eight children, the oldest girl. I had five brothers and two sisters and one of my brothers died, drowned when he was six. But the rest of us are still all around.

Reunited

Miriam: My daughter had given up her son for adoption at age 7. I couldn't bring him up as I had already brought up five and was working out myself. She found him passing out coffee at Tim's when he was 18. That was some reunion! I had always prayed he would be well cared for and he was brought up by very nice people.

Second youngest of eight

Tom Let's talk about family sizes while we're at it. You said you were one of eight?

Ron: Yes.

Tom: How big a spread? Were you among the oldest or youngest?

Ron: Second youngest.

Tom: So they were mostly all older.

Ron: Five girls and three boys.

Tom: Did they take care of you or did they abuse you?

Ron: Oh no, we were all well looked after, you know, and Mom was at home.

Tom: I said 'abuse' facetiously.

Ron: I know.

Tom: Did they dominate your life? Or were you pretty much free?

Ron: Lots of times you didn't get as much to eat as you'd like. We weren't well-off people, that's for sure.

Tina: I think that's par for the course growing up in that time of the century.

Ron: Yes. The women work hard at home doing the laundry. Carrying it out—I remember Mom carrying the clothes in. They still froze.

Tina: I remember carrying in my father's long john's. I could stand 'em up in the corner.

Ron: You raised your own beef and your own pork.

Tina: Yup. And your own chickens.

Ron: Yes, exactly, and we didn't have a lot of land, but enough for that.

Deaf sister

Miriam: We had a sister who was deaf from birth. She didn't go to school, but she was as smart as the rest of us. We talked to her with our own sign language. At age 33 she and my mother were killed in a car accident in 1966.

Having our picture taken

Ethel: I remember my mother dressing us in our Sunday clothes because my aunt was coming home from Charlottetown where she was working and was going to take our pictures. We were so excited! We had bows in our hair and my brother and I were holding a kitten. (I remember someone pulling my hair and I never said a word.) Today I can still remember that day like it was yesterday.

Seamstress

Ruth: My father farmed and also worked at a sawmill some days a week, not far from the homestead. My mother was really a good seamstress and loved to sew for the family and many of the neighbours. She had poor health due to an early childhood accident when she got her neck badly burned with a woollen scarf and a wax candle when getting apples from a cellar tub. She never complained. As a young woman she and her sister worked for 10 years in Quincy, Massachusetts before returning to PEI where she married my father.

My father

Neil: My father, Carl Brydon, was actually born in Charlottetown, Massachusetts, U.S.A., but when he was a year and a half old, his parents returned to Nova Scotia where he grew up. He eventually came back to Boston where he met his wife. After that, they went to Florida where they operated a restaurant. When that didn't go as planned, they came back to the Boston area

He was a hard worker, often working two jobs. He ran a farm and worked besides. One job that he had was working nights in an ice plant. He was a man of few words but saw a lot. There is one trait that he passed on to his children—no patience. Some of his children and grandchildren have the same trait—no patience!

A martyr is my relative

Pat: When I was engaged to my first husband, my sister and I used to work in a little town called Bury St. Edmunds which was in Suffolk in England a very ancient walled City that had gates all around it. There was north gate, south gate, east gate, west gate—well you get the picture—and in the middle was this beautiful Monastery or Abby as they called them and it was free, so you could go in and walk around the gardens—beautiful gardens—and sit on benches and enjoy your lunch or whatever. So my sister and I who worked in the same building used to wander there at lunchtime and sit and enjoy the lovely—well the monks used to walk around and chant. It was very peaceful. We used to look around there and we found a monument which was quite a tall sort of obelisk and on it were names of people who were martyred—it was called a Martyr's Stone and there was names of all the people over all the years of the ancient times who had been martyred for some reason or other—burnt at the stake or whatever. When I was looking at it one day I noticed there was a name on it that I recognized and the name was Potten which was Dutch which was a derivative. And that was the name of the fellow that I was engaged to, so I took him to look at it and sure enough there was Sarah [or Agnes or Joan] Potten so it stuck in my mind,

and over the years I didn't think too much about it, but when I had my 80th birthday, I was in Ottawa visiting all my friends and my daughter who has a house there and we got talking about this one night. They were asking me to reminisce over the years, and I was telling them about that and my daughter said just a minute and she got on the Internet for whatever people do and she discovered this Sarah Potten. She had been burnt at the stake because she possessed a Bible. Now Bibles were not for regular people, so that was one strike against her, plus this Bible was written in English and that was against the rules of the church who said everything had to be written in Latin. It was really interesting to think that all those years went by and we finally discovered this ancestor—on the Internet.

PEOPLE I REMEMBER

My Friend Mrs. Lem

Barbara: We didn't seem to have much in common—she was old and I was young—other than that we both lived on a farm; but we had a bond that was forged when I was very young—just a baby in a crib. I had been mysteriously sick, as babies often are, for a couple of days and my mother decided she had better call the doctor. In those days the doctor made house calls. He came at a very busy time; my mother was cooking the noon hour meal for the workers and the family, and in those days that meant a very full course meal for men who were very hungry from working all morning in the field. I was lying in my crib, just by the kitchen door, so my mother could keep an eye on me, and when the doctor walked in the door he didn't wait for Mum to come over to the crib with him, he just whipped the blanket off me.

Startled, I let out a loud wail, the doctor said "Nothing wrong with her" and left Mum to comfort me and keep watch to the food cooking on the stove.

A couple of hours later, the meal was over, the stove had been allowed to die out, the men had all gone back to the fields, Mum had finished cleaning up and was working on the supper-time meal, and the crib was still beside the kitchen door. Suddenly I went into convulsions.

My mother called to my sister, "Run quickly and get Mrs. Lem."

My sister ran to the farm next door and she and Mrs. Lem came running up the path that connected the farmyards. She took one look, grabbed me from my mother, opened the water tank on the side of the stove and plunked me in, clothes, shoes and all! (The water was cool by then). I know now that the cool water brought my temperature down immediately. I survived the illness, the dunking, and from then on, it was known in my family that Mrs. Lem had saved my life, when the doctor had not even bothered to check me over. The bond was forged.

For the first few years of my life I only saw my saviour when Mum took me to visit, or she came to our house for afternoon tea, but by the time I was four years old, I had developed the habit of slipping away on my mother and heading into forbidden places; the stables to stroke the horses, to the porch roof when I was outraged and ran away from home. The first place Mum would look was always down to Mrs. Lem's. I would run down through the barnyard, avoiding the hen house and the rooster that took particular delight is attacking me whenever I went near, through the field, unlatching the gate between the two farms, past Mr. Lem's barnyard, and into their kitchen where Mrs. Lem would be working away. We would chat for a few minutes, the proverbial cookie would be produced, and we would go out to the well-house where Mrs. Lem would pull up the milk container from the cold waters and pour out a glass of milk for me.

As we chatted, and when my cookie and milk were all gone, she would gently say, "I don't think you told your mother you were coming to see me."

"Who told you?" I would ask.

"Oh—a little bird told me." was her answer. (I silently consigned that darn bird to a terrible end!) "Perhaps you should go home and tell her where you were, she might be worried."

So I would reluctantly set off back for home, knowing full well that my mother should never worry when I was with my friend. It was in later years when I was a mother that I understood that their main fear was the well, which was open and went down about eighty feet!

When I got a little older I would come home from school and tell my mother

Family memories: People I Remember

I was going down to see Mrs. Lem. Their farm had several attractions that we did not have. Of course there was their well in a well house, and when you looked down you could never see the bottom, but oh how cold and smooth was the milk that they kept in milk cans there. There was the separator which I loved to help turn as Mr. Lem poured the buckets of milk into the large bowl. As we turned the handle on the separator the cream would separate from the milk and come out a spout from which hung a shiny metal container and the skim milk would flow out a larger spout into the large milk cans that Mr. Lem shipped to the dairy.

Most interesting of all was the radio, which ran on batteries. It was a little wooden box with two large batteries connected by wires that sat on a table next to the wood stove. When I would get there from school, Mrs. Lem would turn on that radio and the two of us would sit at the table and listen raptly to 'our stories' which were the soap operas of the day that ran for a whole hour. As we listened, *Mr.* Lem reclined on the horsehair couch on the other side of the stove. When the stories were over, we would all stir—me to go home to do chores, Mr. Lem to do some barn work, and Mrs. Lem to cook their supper.

Every so often, Mrs. Lem would ask me to supper! With great anticipation I would run home to ask permission. We would only have simple things, 'cause dinner was at noon, but I would tuck in with great relish and eat everything on my plate, because I knew there was a special treat coming for dessert. After we cleared the plates, Mrs. Lem would emerge from the pantry with my favourite—canned plums! They looked so appetizing—the oil lamp on the table would pick up the deep burgundy colour of the plums and the wonderful syrup in which they rested in the glass dessert bowls. Mr. Lem had a favourite joke he liked to play on unsuspecting innocents. He would say "you are drinking out of the wrong side of the glass; you should drink out of the other side". He did this the first time I remember eating with them, and although I heard Mrs. Lem say, "Now Lem", I wanted my manners to be correct so I tried to drink out of the other side of the glass. Of course the water spilled out and down my front, and Mrs. Lem got annoyed at her husband and made lots of 'tut-tut' noises as she patted me dry, but Mr. Lem had this huge grin on his face, so I knew that this was the expected outcome. But he only got me once.

When her grandchildren came to stay for a week or so Mrs. Lem would take us to the shore to swim in the afternoons, we would pick apples from the wonderful old Transparent trees that grew next to the house, play with the batch of kittens the barn cat delivered in the hayloft, and generally take for granted the summer that was a golden time for us. But I still liked it when school started and I could visit my friend Mrs. Lem in the afternoons and tell her all my trials and troubles and accomplishments. She empathized with me over my troubles, congratulated me on my achievements, and made gentle suggestions when she felt I needed them.

There were a lot of differences between our farm and theirs. We had electricity, so we had light bulbs instead of oil lamps, refrigeration for our food, our water came from taps instead of an open well. But there was something magical about eating by lamplight, listening to a static-y battery radio, and going out to the well for water—tap water will never taste as good. And I would never have a more empathetic friend. I was never just a kid, we talked like equals, and she never judged or had a harsh word for me. She had the kindest eyes I have ever seen.

Unfortunately, just like Johnny Painter and Puff the Magic Dragon, I grew older, and the magic of those years lost their glow as my interests changed. I would still visit once in a while but when we sold the farm and moved further up the road into a bungalow we lost touch. The last time I saw her she was in hospital, and she never came home. She had a name, her name was Sadie, and she had family who loved her, but to me she was, and will always be, my friend, Mrs. Lem.

Grammie MacKenzie

Dora: We used to just come out here on Sundays for a while. Then after Grammie MacKenzie died, we came out to stay—got the house fixed up. We had it wired for her but she wouldn't turn the lights on. She still went upstairs with a lamp.

Arlene: Creature of habit. [chuckle]

Dora: We wanted it wired because we were afraid she'd fall down the steps. But she was in her 83rd year when she died. And here I am up there and don't think nothing about it. [Dora had just celebrated her 86th birthday]

Arlene: That's what keeps you going is those stairs.

Mary: Keeps your heart strong.

ENTERTAINMENT

RADIO AND TV

Our first radio

Veda: The first radio we had, you had to use earplugs and only one person could listen to it at a time. It was like the radios that the kids build—

[voice in the background]: Crystal sets.

Veda: Yeah that was it. That was the first one we had, though eventually we got a radio that had a battery. We didn't have electric power at that time. Of course, once we got power, we got a power radio.

Battery conflict

Tina: You were talking about the radios, and we were in competition with our car! My father had a car. The battery from the car would come into the house when *his* stories were on; as soon as his stories were finished the battery would jump right back into the car so he could go to work. So we were having a short visit with the radio!

Radio programs

Ronda: I was just trying to remember some of the programs we were listening to on the radio. In Charlottetown during the War years we used to get an adventure series called *Alfred Lanky* which was about an aeroplane [with a Canadian air crew] that went on bombing missions over Germany. They made the planes do whatever they wanted to, and every week on Sunday night, we used to sit around a big old radio that sat on the floor. We didn't get really good reception, but we used to sit there and listen to *Alfie Lanky,* which was the adventures of the crew of this Lancaster bomber and for all

the years until after the war ended we'd listen to that.

Another program was Jack Benny. At that time, he was a spokesman for *Jell-O*. He would begin with, "Jell-O again, this is Jack Benny...." Of course, he had all the groups on.

We always listened to *The Lone Ranger*. It was one of our favourite programs. That was before television. The Lone Ranger would come on and who could forget the music from the *William Tell Overture*.

That's about the end of my memories of radio because after the war was over people got televisions and stuff like that.

More radio programs

Richard: Some of the memories of the radio days were the soap operas. *Ma Perkins* was one, you remember [several indistinguishable program names offered in the background] and at noon there was a farm broadcast and *The Gillum's*. They were on everyday and I used to listen to them and then there was another show on Sunday I used to listen to it was called *Hawaii Calls(?)* with Hawaiian music at 1:30 [*Twilight Zone* someone added] and I want to add one our neighbour was always very industrious. But he always had time to enjoy life, so my father and him were working in the woods—they used to trade help in the woods—so when it was 2:30 and he seen him packing up the saws, my father said, "Where are you going this Saturday?

"Oh, I've got to get home to hear me stories."

I mentioned *The Gillum's*. [*Old Ma Perkins* offered by someone in the background] There was an hour of soap operas from 4 to 5 on CBC, I think.

Antigonish was a very interesting station.

Pat: We only got one station that I remember.

Barbara: There was one in the morning....

Richard: Back then there was no FM or AM—everything was AM. CFCY (Charlottetown) was a very popular station and then CJFX from Antigonish was 520 and CBC—I don't know what number it was back then—it was from Halifax that was the one the carried *The Gillum's*. They were a farm family and they were unreal. Angus Gillum was the father and Rob Roy was the son... the memories are coming back—and it was very, very interesting

Barbara: What was the one that was on it was either 8 or 8:30 in the morning and it was *Helen somebody* and she worked in an office—anybody remember? I used to hear it before I went to school... I can't remember her name either.

Richard: Does anybody remember Ches Cooper and Loman MacAuley [Oh Yes, in the background] and who done the show in the evening? Was it Ray Simmons?

Barbara: I believe it might have been, Richard. And then at 4:30 they got modern in the late fifties. They put on a half an hour of rock and roll before the *Outports* came on at 5 o'clock.

[here fell a debate about which programs came on when]

It was just a program of local music.

Pat: yes but don't forget *Don Messer and the Islanders* on Saturday night.

Richard: You must remember that.

Pat: We were surprised to see them all in person. I'd be so busy I wouldn't hear it.

Barbara: I think you're right Richard, I think it was Ray Simmons.

Richard: Remember Jake Leyden(?) and he changed his voice. They called him the old fellow or whatever. He changed his voice went on with the queerest talk you ever heard in your life. And I don't know who Percy Baker was but he'd come on every couple of weeks. He used to sing *The Pride of Glencoe*, remember that?

Barbara: yes, yeah. Remember there was another one. Percy Baker used to sing *Change The Green Laurel To The Red White And Blue*—they used to play that on Antigonish.

Richard: I wonder who Percy Baker was. That wasn't his real name.

Halls of Ivy

Tom: When I was three of four my parents really loved a radio program called *The Halls Of Ivy* with Ronald Coleman. I don't remember much—it didn't make a huge impression except lying on the rug and listening. It was easy to fill in a picture from one's imagination.

Hockey and the mouse

Barbara: This isn't my story—it's my husband's. He and his family had moved to the country because his Dad wanted to raise vegetables and do all those sorts of things—they had a cow and so on and you couldn't do that in Charlottetown. So they moved out to the country. They had an old battery-operated Radio and on Saturday night they used to broadcast the hockey game. The old farmhouse certainly wasn't sealed up for the winter. When the hockey game come on no one talked—it wouldn't have mattered if the house was on fire—no one. So they're all gathered around the radio listening to the game on Saturday night. His father had old woollen socks that his wife used to knit—you know the big heavy socks—and he was sitting there with his ankles crossed, listening to the game very intently and the kids noticed this mouse come out and come over towards him. It climbed up on his toe! They wanted to tell him there was a mouse on his toe, but he would hold up his hand and say, "Nope." There was absolutely no way anyone could speak when the game was on. His father would get all excited at scoring a goal and bump his hand on his knee and the mouse would go up in the air and land back down again. This went on for about half an hour. The rest of them were in stitches and couldn't even listen to the hockey game. Finally it was the end of the game and he turned off the radio and saw one of the boys looking at the mouse. His father said, "Well!" and kicked the mouse up to the ceiling and it fell down stone dead.

First sight of a TV

Winnie: I'd left Toronto with Audrey and her fiancé, and on the way along we stopped at a pub in Burlington, and they said, "Everyone's 21."

I said, "I'm not 21."

"If anyone asks you, you're 21. You don't have to drink." It was the Pig and Whistle. "You can have a glass of Coke or whatever."

So I went into the pub and took a seat and looked up and there, on a shelf, was a television. I had never seen one except in pictures in magazines. Wow.

Entertainment: Radio and TV

The movies in that little square thing! Oh my goodness!

Later, when I was married, we didn't have a television. Not everyone had them then. They were fairly new. I remember being in the hospital for our first child, and the girls talking about different shows that they had watched, and I didn't know what they were talking about. We didn't have a television.

"You don't have a television?!"

My god, I thought, since we had running water and an inside toilet, we were way up in the world—I didn't need a television. Finally we bought one—a little Admiral—a little portable thing. It cost $89 and it used to sit on the floor. I remember Saturday morning programs. The children would watch *Captain Kangaroo* and *The Little Rascals* and they would watch that you know, 15 or 20 minutes. You could get a lot of work done in the meantime, 'cuz they were glued to the television.

TV and the loss of innocence

Tom: In my youth, I always felt underprivileged in comparison with my friends. I don't think we got a television until sometime in the early 1950s even though my father was an electrical engineer. Television, when we finally got one, was black-and-white of course. A colour set in my family didn't come until after I'd left home in the mid 60s. I do remember around 1955 in Arlington Heights in Illinois that we would move and set tray tables in front of the television and eat dinner watching the Wednesday-night Disney program—*World of Disney* or whatever (I forget what it was called in the early days). That one program we got to watch. I do remember that they had Davy Crockett with Fess Parker, and then there was the Alamo. I don't remember all the details, but I do remember that in my school there was a boy named David Crockett and he actually got on local television. It was the rage to have a coonskin cap or at least a tail. I don't know if they were real or were just synthetic. Those are my memories of radio and television.

Somewhere in there I remember Saturday-morning westerns. I think it was the *Lone Ranger*, but what most remember now was the time I began to realize was that the horseback chase scenes began to look very similar from week to week. The *same* rock feature would go by multiple times, with the *same* posse or bad guys galloping by. Perhaps that was the beginning of a critic's spirit in evaluating movies.

Music

Family music times

Dora: Our house was always open to everyone, and there was hardly a meal without someone extra.

Most of us were musical—we could play or sing. Some played the piano, banjo and the fiddle and Sunday nights was always a sing-song. It was a wonderful time.

Kids in the background

Mary: So did you have music every night after supper or was it a big deal on Saturday nights?

Dora: Anytime *Don Messer and the Islanders* were on, we had a dance. And of course we all played games, with my brothers and the whole works of us.

My father and mother used to go to the different homes and have dances, just a group of them. My Dad would take his slippers under his arm; they'd be going to a neighbour's place to have a little dance, which wouldn't happen very often.

Arlene: My Dad came from a musical family. They would go to different homes and play cards and then the music would start. And all the kids would go in one room and they were told they could sleep.

Mary: [laughing] And they'd play cards instead, would they?

Arlene: Well, I don't remember that. I was the youngest, my brother was the oldest and then there was my sister, and they remember that.

Dancing

Dora: We all had our chores to do. And we always had our supper at five o'clock because *Don Messer and the Islanders* were on and this was important to us. We'd push the old table back and we all went through an old time set, my brother calling off the dance. My mother and father both, we all joined in the dance.

Never too old to learn

Richard: I've reached the point—course there's a lot of gall involved—where I am on the stage in Rollo Bay playing the violin. Last year...

Barbara: At the Rollo Bay Fiddle Festival?

Richard: ...and again this year we're playing [Sardina?].

Barbara: Richard!

Tom: Actually? Or in your imagination?

Barbara: He doesn't *have* an imagination! For real! [laughter]

Richard: My imagination is not that wild. I've been taking fiddle—when you first picked up the violin, there's no way you say you're ever gonna be able to play. Now I can't play without notes.

Barbara: Good.

Richard: But I can play some tunes with the notes ahead of me. But in this group, I know when they're gonna change. I know the tune in my head, and I'm not putting anybody off key so, as I say, it's 75% gall...

Tom: Well that you've probably got!

Richard: Why that's what I got as far as the fiddle is concerned.

Barbara: You play with Amy Swenson's group?

Richard: No. But Lorraine [his wife] was. But then I had the benefit of having a fiddler for a wife, which is a big help. I wouldn't be on the stage only for her.

Barbara: Well that's good. What group do you play with?

Richard: The Morell group. There was 14 or 15 of us.

Pat: When are we going to go out and see 'em play?

Richard: We're going to be in Rollo Bay on Saturday evening, and we're playing at a church in St. Peters—I'm not sure which church it is. It's one of the churches there. That's on a Friday evening the last of June.

OTHER ENTERTAINMENT

Across the ice to the movies

Corena: I also remember that the first movie I ever saw was at the Old Georgetown Theatre—that was the one that burned—and Bruce Yo had come down from Montague to show movies. I don't remember the name of the movie, but I sure remember what a big deal it was to go in the horse and sleigh—the box sleigh—over to Georgetown.

Tom: So you were talking about going over for ice cream...

Corena: ...and also the movie. Mom and Dad—my mother and father and my brother—my brother was three years younger than I and the four of us going over in the box sleigh. I think it was called that. I was going over in the horse and sleigh...

Tom: Around or on the ferry?

Corena: No, on the ice. Now in the wintertime they would—they called it 'tree the ice'. They would put these bushes on so that, if a storm came up while you were out there, you would be able to find your way back. And of course, the horses and sleigh, when we got to Georgetown, there was a big shed open-ended where you drove the horse and sleigh in and walked to the theatre. We had one of those sheds in Lower Montague, close to where the cemetery is today—there was a shed there, too.

Disneyland roller coaster

Pat: The scariest ride I can ever remember was Space Mountain in Disneyland. I could barely stand up when I got off. I thought I was going to have a heart attack. It was terrifying.

Tom: Yeah I remember when my son was little we also went to Disneyland. We went on some sort of a new ride that was still in the debugging stage. It was a water ride and some safety thing tripped. Everyone had to walk out, so they gave us a free priority pass to any ride in the park. So we cut into line for Space Mountain. What a shock! You sat in this seat in the pitch black—

couldn't see a thing, and lighted things came at you from nowhere. You had no idea where you were and if you were going to go up or down or sideways.

I just remember asking myself, "Why would anybody in their right mind *pay* to be tortured like that?" Needless to say I'm not much of a rides person myself.

Pat: There was a space there where it came to a dead halt. It was all black, so you didn't know what was happening, and all of a sudden it went straight down. Okay. Just before you get on there was a sign that said, *Anybody With Severe Heart Problems Should Not Go On This Ride.* Now we know why.

Tina: You wouldn't have gotten me on it because I was having heart problems.

Comics and wishes

Tom: My parents never spent money on luxuries or even what I wished were necessities. The proof of that was the case of comic books. There were ones that cost 10¢ and then there were the really fat 25¢ ones. I can't remember the number of times I secretly lusted after the fat ones. Some of my friends had parents who let them have whatever they wanted.

It wasn't so much that my parents would say, "No, you can't have it."

It was just that you kind of didn't feel good about asking for things like that. Somehow they weren't necessities. The attitude must have been implanted in early childhood. I do remember, from the rare indulgence, my picture of the world coming through comic books. There were Huey, Dewey, and Louie and Uncle Scrooge. In the comic books they would have adventures in Far Corners of the World. I think most of my knowledge of geography and foreign cultures came from those comic books. I don't know about the accuracy of a comic book, but there it was.

In later years I recall in school the Weekly Reader and/or Scholastic Book Club. A flyer was passed out that described books you could buy. Money had to be turned in with your order, and a few weeks later the books would come. Again I felt limited in the freedom of what I could afford. Even today, when I find such books in used-book stores I end up purchasing them.

WORK & JOBS

FARMING

Farm tasks

Mary Ellen: I lived on a farm near Bear River with my Dad, John Joseph MacKinnon, and my mother, Ellen Adele (Fisher) MacKinnon and step-sister and step brothers. Mom had 5 children in her second marriage. On the farm we had milking cows, pigs, hens and roosters. There were three horses to work the land on the farm, as well as haul wood from the woods. Dad put in a garden and potatoes.

Automated Churn

Pat: My folks only had a couple of cows and this was during the war and the process was, they milked the cows and then they put it in this little container which they called a creamer, which was about 2 feet high and it had a little window down the side. What they would do, they would hook it to a cable or chain and lower it down the old well which was unused. That worked very well. In the evening, before the next milking, we would crank the whole thing back up and put it on the counter—table at the time—hold the spout and watch the cream come down, and then you stopped when it got past the cream, so you got this wonderful cream.

My foster mother used to make butter. The process was kind of labour-intensive because you just cranked over this little crank, but my foster father was very enterprising he had a friend who was a blacksmith. This blacksmith made a little container to go over the spindle of the washing machine. So you took out the vanes and you popped this little container and just plugged it in and away you went. In no time at all you had butter. Of course you're supposed to take it in to the dairy because it was rationed and just have a certain amount but nobody bothered with that. [laughter]

Pat: But it was fun. After the butter was made she put it in this little sort of square wooden container and patted it all down and washed it a little. It had a little design on the top so you got this neat little pat of butter with this little daisy design on the top. Now how about that!

Barbara: I still have the paddles for making the design.

Tom: Can you talk some more about this automated churn that you had?

Pat: It was a very old fashioned washing machine but it was electric.

Tom: You had electricity then?

Pat: Yes.

Barbara: Was it a roller type?

Pat: No. It was just the vanes and the clothes went back and forth, back and forth, inside the washing machine, and you put them through the wringer. Everybody had a ringer and then you put them on the clothesline. We didn't have a dryer. This would now be an old washing machine, but then it was considered quite modern. For churning you took the spindle out of it—or the vanes that fit over the spindle—so you exposed the spindle and this churn-thing just slipped right on over the spindle. You plugged the washer in and away it went, back and forth, back and forth, and in no time at all you had butter.

Milking and milk processing

Veda: Well, I don't have too much about cream. My grandparents they had a herd of Jersey cows which gave lots of cream. They separated it and they had a cold room. It was below ground and it had a roof over it and that's where they kept everything cold. They kept all their cold stuff in it. My grandmother made jam and it went down to the cold room. At home we had a herd of cattle, and we sold whole milk to Charlottetown—Father and two other men in the district—they took turns, except there was none on Sunday, and they hauled the milk to Charlottetown, whoever's turn it was. As soon as they milked the cows the milk went into milk cans and it was put in a trough of water. We had a motorized pump that supplied the water to this tank—it had to be kept cold 'till it went to Charlottetown. The pump also supplied our house.

Tom: So you had pressure water. You didn't have to pump.

Veda: No.

Barbara: I'm not sure what you said when you were talking about the cream—I've kind of got sidetracked for a minute there. Did you say what you did with the cream after?

Veda: No, I forgot that part but it was the same as she said—they made butter. I didn't finish my story about the cream. My grandmother churned it into butter. Their churn had a paddle that went up and down, and when we visited in the summer time—my sister and I—we thought it was great fun helping to make the butter.

Barbara: Did you sell the butter or keep it?

Veda: I don't know that. They used it. I don't know if they sold it besides that. I wasn't very old to remember.

Brief butter business

Barbara: I could tell you a story about butter—not actually about cream. We also had cows on the farm but my Dad did mixed farming so we didn't have a cream license. What do you call it, Richard, where you sold the cream and they came around and collected it?

[background]: Quota, maybe.

Barbara: Well there were people on other farms—it was a totally agricultural district I lived in. Some of them raised milk cattle and they had a cream quota, so they would have to separate the milk into the cream and the skim milk, but we just had only had 6 cows so the milk we collected was mainly for our own use, and we also used to feed it to the animals. Half a mile down the road from my house there's a wharf and a lot of boats used to come in and we would ship vegetables and things. One thing they wanted along with potatoes and turnips and everything else was butter, so one day my Dad came home and he was quite happy to relate that he had acquired the franchise—for want of a better word—of supplying the boats—and I say boats, plural—with butter. Of course my mother was the one that made butter not my father and the farm hands—they were out in the field. So my mother was not terribly amused because at that time we had a churn and it stood about 2½ or 3 feet high, and had a wooden plunger and it was a long stick with a cross piece across the bottom. You had to stand there all day and plunge this thing up and down until finally you'd check in and look and you'd see the little bits of butter forming on top, and then you'd keep her going for another little while and then you knew you had to stop at one point and collect all the butter together. What was left over was the buttermilk. We also had a cold well and Dad used to save the buttermilk and put it in jugs down in the cold well. My goodness, on a hot summer day that cool buttermilk with little tiny bits of butter floating around in it was the most delicious thing. Anyway my mother had to churn and I had to churn and my sister had to churn and we churned and churned.

Finally my mother said, "Nope. I've had enough with this churn. You'll going to have to let someone else supply the butter to the boats."

That was the end. He was rather disappointed because it was quite a lucrative business in the days on the farm when there wasn't a lot of money going around, but it was just way too much for one or two people to do. So that's my story about butter.

Cream, butter and a ploughing match

Barbara: You know, getting back to this cream business, remember the cream cans? We really didn't separate because we only had six cattle but my neighbour had cattle and he had a cream quota and every evening the cream truck would come around and pick up the cream. We used to have to take it down to the bottom of the road—I say 'we' because I was always sticking my nose in my neighbour's business when I was a little kid and he very patiently tolerated me around the barn and around the house. I would go down while they were separating, and when they separated—and I still have a working separator at home—yeah it works—we used to separate and the cream would come out first, out of one spout and then the milk would come out of another, so the cream can held *only* the cream and the other got the milk the skim milk. They had a well—it was probably about 60 feet deep. They used to put the cream cans on a rope and put them down the well and they would keep them there and keep them cold until the truck came around. You knew what day it was coming so then you'd lift up the cream cans and horse and cart them down to the bottom of the lane and then wait for the truck to pick them up.

I do have a working separator and we used to do a demonstration at the Dundas ploughing match—my husband and I—we got milk—whole milk—from a farmer in Dundas and I turned the crank and we gathered the cream and the milk and it came out separate and we'd do a demonstration twice a day at the ploughing match and everyone would come and watch.

At the end of it I'd say, "Here are some of the products you get from milk."

We had butter and we had buttermilk and I had homemade ice cream that I had made the night before. What they didn't know was that I went to the store and got the cream and make the ice cream. There were line-ups out of that huge barn all the way at the end of the barn and back for this homemade ice cream, and we'd put it in these little cups like they put coleslaw in in restaurants. Before that children would never know where butter or ice cream or anything came from. We had a lot of fun.

Then they shut us down. They thought we were using real milk that hadn't been pasteurized, but we weren't.

Ice cream and hail

Veda: In the line of ice cream I can tell you a story. One summer when I was at my grandparents, just up the other end of the Island in Montrose, just beyond Alberton, they had this terrible hail storm and great big hailstones. A girl was caught out in it and she was really an awful mess after. When it was all over my grandparents, they gathered up the hailstones, and of course they already had cream because that's what they did with their milk, separated it. And they made some homemade ice cream. And it was the best thing I ever tasted. Used hailstones for it.

[various]: I'll be darned

Veda: It just covered the ground. They were about that big around [no record of her gesture was saved].

Barbara: What was your parent's name—your grandparents in Montrose?

Veda: Pridham

Barb: I know a lot of Pridhams up there today.

Dairy farming and creameries

Richard: A couple of things I want to add about the advantage of electricity when it came to separating the cream. You had to separate by hand, so then

Work & jobs: Farming

we got an electric separator, it was a really big step up the ladder and saved a lot of hard work. Then another advantage of having electricity, among many, was we got a milking machine. [ah] There was a lot of advantages having electricity on the farm as well as in the house.

Richard: Another thing I forgot to add was the value of the skim milk. It was fed to the calves. It was considered very valuable. If we had a surplus, it was fed to the hogs. And speaking about cream, my father used to haul cream—there was a factory in New Perth. There were several factories, and New Perth was one we used to haul. There was three or four more, I can't just remember. There was one in Eldon, and I used to go with them when there wasn't school and gather bottles and sell them at the store. There was a store in New Perth.

Tom: Is that what you would call a Creamery then?

Richard: Yup. The cream cans had to be steamed, so that was my job steaming the cans at the factory. People used to send for butter, and I remember the ration tickets in war time. They'd have to send their ration tickets—put them on the cream can at the gate and they were only allowed so much butter, and we used to drop off the butter. Anybody that knew they were getting butter used to get out—summertime they'd be out soon as the cream can would come because the butter would melt.

Pat: Does anybody remember the Crapaud Creamery?

Barbara: You could still get Crapaud Butter until a few years ago.

Richard: You remember New Perth? Bruce Myers lives there now.

Pat: When I was young of course the Crapaud Creamery was in full production

and for years that was the only butter I bought, and then we moved to New Brunswick when my husband got another job and we couldn't get it in New Brunswick, so every time we knew somebody that was going to the Island we would always put in our order Crapaud Creamery Butter. You can still buy it?

Barbara: Well, until a few years ago. It closed down, didn't it, Richard?

Richard: Nathan Dewar it was one of the originators, and his father, John A. Dewar.

Milking

Pat: I can see my Dad milking the cows by hand and the cats would be sitting there waiting and he would turn the teat and squeeze it and the cat would grab it. We had three or four cats he would always aim the cats always managed to open their mouth. They tried to teach me to milk one day but I couldn't get at it and my Dad was a sort of sly smile, "You have to learn how to turn the cow on." I never quite knew how to turn the cow on, so I wasn't much good at it.

Barb: I tried to milk cows too, but because the farmer, Mr. Stet, who had the Ayrshires, he'd still milk cows by hand. I tried to do it once, but he'd do the same thing with the cats and I couldn't turn them on—didn't know how to turn them on.

Pat: I had visions of putting the pail underneath and getting the tail.

[?]: That's only in cartoons.

Barbara: The cats and the farmers were a great partnership because the cats kept the mice down and the rats in the barn and the farmer in turn gave the cats milk so it is a two-way relationship. They both valued one another quite a bit.

Tom: Cattle with horns—were they dangerous? [everyone: No, no]

Richard: You didn't dehorn milk cows.

Barbara: The cows today, they look strange.

Barb: Beef cattle they never have horns. They cut them off. The Herefords we had they never had horns. I can remember dehorning them. Oh that was awful. These big clippers and blood would squirt up in the air.

[?]: We don't want to hear about it—I'm very sensitive.

Richard: Not a nice job.

Farm jobs

Barb: When I was growing up my Dad was a salesman and he wasn't home very often and we had horses, so we always had to live somewhere where we could board them or keep them. So my Mom got a job as a hired hand for a farmer had a dairy farm just across the road from us. He had cattle—Ayrshires. They had all their horns—he didn't cut their horns off. They were beautiful. A lot of times, if Mom was busy or if Dad wasn't home, we would just stay at the farm—they were. I remember having breakfast there in the morning and we would have porridge and there'd be milk—would have globs of cream in it 'cause they didn't have a separator. I didn't like the clot... no... no! She cooked on a wood stove—she didn't have an electric stove. She made her own donuts. They had maple syrup...

Barbara: Umm, real maple syrup.

Barb: They had a horse that pulled the stone boat because that time of the year the woods would always be muddy, muddy. A stone boat is like a flatbed with no wheels on it. You pull it along.

Barbara: Like a drag?

Barb: We would use that to collect stones. When I farmed with my late husband, we called it a stone boat 'cause we would go in the field and collect stones.

Tom: After you ploughed?

Barb: I don't know how many times I'd be discing and they would get a rock big enough that would be in the discs and I couldn't get them out.

Richard: A rocky area, wasn't it?

Barb: It was Kent County in south-western Ontario. Our farm was sandy and had a band of clay going through it. But, yeah, there were a lot of rocks. That's about two different places I've lived in my life.

Richard: Those Ayrshires, did they separate the cream or what did they ship?

Barb: Oh, they just shipped the cans of milk. I don't remember if they separated them. For the house they probably did. They would ship the milk. Because we didn't have a bus (the only people who got to ride the bus were the high school kids), we had to either walk to school or get a ride. When we could, we would ride on the back of the truck and sit on the milk cans. Once my brother fell right off the truck! Bump!

Crops

Richard: I will talk about grain. In the first early years, we had a broadcast seeder pulled by one horse. When loaded with three to four bags, it would sow 1½ acres, more or less. After that, the seed had to be covered with spring toothed harrows, followed by a drag harrow or pie harrow to smooth over the field. Some harrows had a roller that was a round wooden log, shaped with a seat and hauled by one horse.

Potato growing back then was all by hand. The land was prepared similar to grain only deeper. The seed potatoes had to be cut by hand, and people were doing the cutting—usually in the kitchen. The sets (seeds) were put in baskets, and then dumped into bags to take to the field. Once there, they were dumped back into baskets. The field was marked with a wooden marker, four drills at a time, thirty-four to thirty-six inches apart. The seed (sets) were dropped eight to ten inches apart by the workers, and this was followed by a horse-hoe used to cover and make the drill. The next development in potato planting was called *tuber unit* where the potatoes were carried in a sack hanging from the planters' shoulder. The idea was to plant all the pieces of a tuber in one place so in case of disease it would be contained in one place. This was an easier way of cutting and planting all done in the field. After that the mechanical planter was introduced, hauled by a tractor, planting two rows at a time. This machine was updated to one which would plant four or six rows and also cut the sets. Today they are equipped with computers which help to keep the rows straight and the depth even.

Before long, the weeds would start in the potato field, and a horse-drawn scuffler would be towed between the rows. This scuffler had handles with six shears on it cutting the weeds. When the green leaves of the potatoes showed above the ground this scuffler would be brought out again with a larger drill to keep the soil up around the growing potato plants. Spraying would begin as soon as the bugs appeared. DDT was the spray we used, put into hand-pumped sprayers, mounted in the dump cart. This cart was hauled by two horses. Depending on the conditions, we also had to spray for blight. In those days it was a two-wheeled sprayer with a forty-five gallon or more drum mounted with a hand pump. You pumped as the horse pulled the machine through the drills two at a time. The bigger growers had a power unit run by the turning of the wheels.

We also grew turnips, usually in one to five acres. Cultivation was similar to other crops; the drills had to be set thirty inches apart. The rows had to be flattened by the roller and planted by a turnip seeder that was pushed by hand, dropping the seeds all along the rows. When the turnips were anywhere from two to four inches high, thinning was done with a hand-held hoe, leaving one plant every four to six inches. Weeds were also taken out as well as the unneeded turnips.

We also grew strawberries, which involved a lot of hand labour. The strawberry plants were planted by hand about one foot apart, in rows three feet apart. There was a lot of weeding later on, and the runners had to be covered with soil to make new plants for the second year. Several people had to be hired to pick the berries and we sold them at a strawberry exchange in Charlottetown located at the site which is now the Red Shores race track. There was a cold storage in Montague run by a Johnston couple as well.

We grew corn for the cattle, planted by hand in rows, as well as kale, which was another choice for fall feeding. The first crop to come in was the hay. It was cut with a two-horse hay mower and put in windrows by a one-horse dump rake—usually my job in those days. Forks were used to stack the hay into bales, then onto the wagons. The hay was then hauled to the barnyard where it was raked once more, into large haystacks to be hauled into the barn lofts later on. This was hard work, done on very warm days and all by hand.

Experiences in barns

Tom: Can you talk about what it was like climbing, whatever kids did in a barn? What as kids did a barn mean to you?

[?]: A playground.

Tom: Who wants to talk about barn as a playground?

Veda: I can't remember playing in the barn but I *worked* in the barn. I helped milk the cows

[?]: Did you know how to turn the milk on? [joke from earlier conversation]

Veda: Yeah, I did.

Tom: What is the secret?

Veda: I don't know. It's all in the way....

Anyway when I was older after I left home I went back one summer and I could not do it. I had lost the knack of it. My father grew turnips and in the fall when we came home from school every day, the horse and cart would be waiting for us to go back to field and pick up all the turnips and take them home and throw them in the barn. That was our after-school job up until supper time. They use the turnips to feed to the cows. We had some kind of machine that sliced them. The turnips went into it and you turned the handle. The sliced turnips come out. We helped with the hay in the summer time—or at least I did. They had a big hay fork on one end of the barn, and that went down into the load of hay and on the other end of the barn was the horse was hitched up to some sort of apparatus and you had to walk him along until the hay got to the right place in the barn. Somebody yelled and told you to stop. My sister wouldn't do it because she didn't like horses. She was afraid of them she said they always stepped on her. So it was always my job in the summertime in haying to walk the horse.

Tom: Did the horse get so he'd hear and stop?

Veda: No they weren't that smart.

Work & jobs: Farming

More on hand milking

Tom: Who else would like to talk about playing in the barn or working in the barn?

Tina: I've done it all my life. When I was ten my parents had gone visiting and they had left me in charge of the babies. That was fine and when it came to milking time they didn't get back. So I put the two babies into their carriages and brought them into the barn with me and started on milking. They were all milked by hand. First one I milked she gave me about two quarts in the bucket and I figured that that's not right—my mother used to get half a bucket. How come I only got two? So I put the pail away, went and got another pail, started the next one, same thing. Then it dawned on me—they didn't like my fingernails. I had long nails.

Pat: Obviously you knew how to turn [the milk] on, which was a step up from me.

Tina: It wasn't hard to turn them on. My mother showed me how to start milking them 'cause sometimes she couldn't do it and she let me to finish them.

Pat: Do you suppose it's too late for us to learn this?

Barbara: Would you want to, Pat? You'd have to find a cow.

Barb: And there's none on the job where I live.

Richard: They [the cows] would kick you right out of the barn if you tried.

[general consensus]: Oh yeah.

Barbara: We had one that was kind of dirty like that. It would wait until the bucket was half full and then *zoom* give it a kick.

Tina: Not only that. You had to tie the tail up too. If you didn't you'd get slapped in the face with it too. You had to tie the tail to her leg.

Barbara: It's a wonder we survived, Richard.

[?]: We all did—we all survived our childhood.

Tom: Those who didn't aren't here.

Pat: We didn't have all the safety regulations that we have now.

Barbara: Just like in Ontario where you're not allowed to sell unpasteurized milk.

Tina: So after I finished milking the best I could, I knew I'd have to tell Mother how much I got from each one. They got home when I was doing the last one. So my mother started where I'd quit for each one and finished the milking, but she didn't get much because that was too late already. So she missed half of the milk run and the cream. In the meantime, when she took over that one, I went and put it in the separator and separated the milk from the cream. I spent quite a bit of time—it all has to be done by hand. I knew what the work was to going to be for the following day which would be for me sitting there. You had one of these big jugs—a 5 gallon jug—sort of an oval shape with a plunger which went through a hole. It had a cover and it had a hole and you had to put the plunger in first and then put the cover down on top of it, Then you spent all day—you sat there—with half an hour off for lunch. Unless you made sandwiches, you did it while you were plunging there, making butter. I spent the whole day. With all the milk we had I got about two pounds of butter. It had to be taken to the well because we kept it in a cold well. It was a nice cold well but it didn't have a building on. It was just a box over the top of the well and that's where the butter was kept and the milk and anything else meats that we had bought and stuff like that all went down there to keep cool and keep from spoiling.

Barbara: It went down to the frost line so of course you always had the cold coming up from the bottom. That's what kept it cold.

Richard: After the creameries all went out of business we sold whole milk. We had the electric coolers—we had electricity, but some people took their cans to the brook all night. The next door neighbour did that. That held it.

Tina: We didn't do that because all six neighbours around us had electricity; we didn't have any 'cause the property we were on was in charge of the church, so we didn't have any say about whether we got electricity or not. That was the community that did that.

Richard: The last factory we shipped to was Morell, I forgot about that, and Bruce Greene used to haul. There was other drivers too.

Tina: So our cream was shipped once a week to the company in Winnipeg and they came and picked it up and we had to have to have it ready. They dropped off a can when they picked ours—we had our name on it. There were three cans which were changed on certain days. As far as milk went, we never shipped the milk [just the cream]. That was used on the farm because they didn't want skim milk. So that was part of my growing up, and no playing in the barn.

Work & jobs: Farming

By the time I was if 12—you remember they used to have steel wire to tie together the bales of hay that went up in the haymow. That's what we had and they were heavy—twice as heavy as what they are now—and I used to have to help push them up to the second floor.

Richard: By hand?

Tina: By hand—no elevator. I had a ladder leaned against the second floor, and I'd push [the bale] up until it was up and then I'd slip down and climb the ladder and put it way at the back end. That's what I mean—I wasn't playing in the barn. I was working. Whenever I left the barn I said, "That's it."

Richard: You'd need gloves on—the wire would tear the hands off you.

Tina: Oh yeah. I never did them bare hands. I couldn't work with gloves but that was the only place that I worked with gloves on. And I did that every fall. I was out on the tractor in the spring time. I didn't have a childhood from the time I reached ten.

Farm machinery

Richard: In my many years as a farmer, I believe my generation has seen the most changes in agriculture.

Then there is the farm equipment. My first experience with ploughs was a single sod plough that had a long double blade and two long (handles) shafts. It was hitched to a horse and driven by the farmer. It would only plough one furrow, which made for long days in the spring. All the farm equipment was horse-driven back  then. It was a big step up when the gang plough came along. It was a two-sod plough with levers to set the depth of the furrows, wheels for ease of movement, and pulled by a team of horses.

Another necessity on the farm was the wheel harrows, which had discs to cut the ploughed sod, also hauled by a team of horses. It had a seat for the farmer. The spring-toothed harrows were half circle spring teeth, used following the whole harrows.

We had livestock too, milk cows, sows, and hens. Milking was done by hand back then. I got a milking machine in later years, which was two units.

We got our first tractor—a Ferguson, for $1500, which was quite a step up from the horses, but we still used the horse machinery like the hay mower, manure spreader. Then we went to machines for the tractor plough, the harrows, cutting bars for the hay. Then we went for the machinery made for the tractor: ploughs, harvesters, cutting bars for the hay, combine for the grain. We were still growing potatoes, with the digger hooked up to the tractor which took two people. We discontinued potatoes and turnips when I took over the farm.

With the milk cows, you had to install bulk tanks and pipe lines. Being by myself then, I remodelled the cattle barn for beef cattle—loose housing. When the cattle were tied indoors, the stable had to be cleaned every day; it was all done by hand—forks and shovels. In winter we hauled the manure to the field, forked it off into a pile from the horse & sleigh to be spread in the spring again. At that time, it had to be forked into the spreader, with three people forking and sometimes four. This was done when the conditions suited; otherwise it was forked out to a pile to be spread later out of the end of the barn. The cattle pens were also forked by hand. Later I made it so I could bring the tractor in with a rear end bucket with loose housing. I cleaned out the manure shed twice a year with the tractor. I retired having sold to the younger boy next door.

Equipment changes included combines which cut and threshed the grain; hay balers and hay cutters and conditioners which helped to dry the hay faster. If I were farming today, the combine would have an air-conditioned cab to keep it cool to do 100 acres a day.

There were many changes in hay making in my early years. After cutting, it was raked into windrows, and sometimes we would put it in coils—they were called that—if it was looking like rain. The bales could withstand the rain. Other changes were the mechanical hayfork (a track in the barn) with a hay carrier on wheels. The fork was dropped into the full hay wagon and the lift was pulled by one horse—usually a big rope or cable—up to the big door and into the loft. The men in the loft would yell when they wanted the rope to be relaxed, and the fork was pulled into the barn to release the hay. Then the fork was let go to run down the rope for another load while the hay was forked back further in to the barn. We also used the hay fork for stacking. We used two 30' poles, erected in a (triangle) shape with a puller top and bottom. A horse was again used to hoist the hay up, and then the square hay-baler was used. We hired people to bale before we owned a baler. We were amazed at the amount of hay you could store in the same space. We then bought a small Ford baler. Help was needed to handle the bales. First they were dropped behind the baler, next we made a straight sleigh hooked on behind. One man would be on the sleigh with a stick put in the ground and then push them off. After that there was a hay buncher, with a trip rope. Ten to twenty were let out. We then got smarter and had the hay wagon attached to the baler. Then it came into the wagon from the baler. A long escalator took the bales into the loft where they were stacked by hand. By then I had a New Holland—a real baler. When the *round* baler came along, I hired one while I farmed. By then there was no hand labour—it was all tractor.

Potatoes farming too was all mechanized. There was no hand labour—except to pick off some stones, etc.

Antique farm equipment

Richard: There's a lot of antique farm machinery now. The first house on the left, after you pass Busters in Cherry Valley—did you ever notice that old Binder out there in that fellow's yard.

Tom: No. Are we talking east or west—up-hill or down?

Richard: When we turn at Cherry Valley, going toward Charlottetown, it's downhill a little bit. And I was talking about the field of grain they had there. They'd stook it in the old way and then they'd thrash it.

They have a 'Thrashing Bee' at Orwell Corner every year. I'm not into [visiting] that 'cause I went through all that hardship and I don't want to see it again. [laughter]

Tom: Why would anybody do it now?

Richard: The younger generation, I guess....

Sugar beets

Tina: When I was 9 years old. I was busy weeding the summer garden. The next week I was going to weeding the Winter Garden. Summer garden is for vegetables like tomatoes, cucumbers, lettuces, etc. Winter Garden is for potatoes, carrots, turnips, onion sets, etc. These are for storing for the winter in the cellar.

Summer garden is also for pickling. When I came home for supper I was asked if I wanted go to work in the sugar beet fields. This would be extra money for clothing and some food. Yes, I would like to help. I had to hurry with my potatoes in the winter garden. Dad's cousin had a field of sugar beets to be weeded. This was only Thursday. That would give me time to finish both the gardens.

Sugar beets were grown all over Manitoba by some farmers. Some had rows ¼ mile long while other fields were ½ mile long. The former had 11 rows to weed while the latter had 6 rows.

The owner of the sugar beet fields was going to pick us up on Monday morning at 6 am. Work started at 7 am…

It took almost an hour to get to the field that we were going to work. We all got into the box at the back of the truck except Mother and Nick, the baby. We had to bring our lunch and snacks and toys for the younger children. My two older brothers, Mother, and I would be working until 5 pm. Then the truck would take us all back home. We always had 1 hour for lunch and 15-minute breaks morning and afternoon. We worked there for one month.

Word got around that we weeded beets. There was some work for us. The pay was good! Every one got a pair of new shoes.

In the fall Dad was asked if my older brothers and I would like to top he beets. The beets were dug up by a team of horses pulling a digger. The beets were dropped on the ground on the field. Every two rows of beets were moved by blade (wooden) so that there was a place to put the beets after the tops were cut off. This was a hard job since some were up to 10 lbs.

The knives we used were very sharp with a hook on the end of the blade. The blade was about 12" long. The fall that we topped the beets it was getting cold, but once you started to work you warmed up quickly.

I took mostly the smaller beets while my oldest brother took the bigger ones. It was a lot of hard work but we needed clothes for school.

We also had another field of beets to hoe across the street, ¼ mile away. We always went home for lunch but took our snacks with us. The field had ¼ mile rows and there were not too many weeds. Again, Mother, Abe, Bill and I were doing the weeding. Ann was playing with the younger boys. At first they wanted to go home because they could see the house. Also they wanted to get other toys. I told them that at lunch we would go home, so they could get a different toy each. We took a wooden box for all the toys they already had on the field...it would keep the toys in the same place. After that I got the box put into the little red wagon so they could pull it to the field. A good idea—we could also carry our lunch in the wagon. It was a lot easier.

Some of the older boys from the region started to work in this field too since the school allowed time off. It was more fun on the break times. That was the only time we got together. Some of the boys and girls from further away came to work on bicycles, but the ones nearby walked just like we did. I was the only one who had to also baby sit. But our boys listened to me, and if they needed something they would come to me.

There were no tractors, cars, or trucks allowed on the field The only time the children were allowed to go on the road was when it was time to go to the field or to go home.

It was a lot of work, but this field we did not have to cut the tops off in the fall because the farmer had bought a machine to do the topping.

This was how I spent my summer. When the hoeing of the beets was done it was time to go back to the gardens—checking for weeds, heaping potatoes, canning yellow beans, tomatoes, and tomato juice, as well as pickling yellow beans, green relish, cucumbers, red ketchup, etc. Then back to school again.

Harvest meals at grandmother's

[editor's note: While Tina grew up on the prairies, the processes and steps she describes were just as true for PEI]

Tina: The summer I was 12, we all went to visit my Grandmother on my mother's side of the family. My uncles were busy getting the harness, wagons, and machines ready for harvesting, and my father went to help there while my mother and I helped with the baking—cakes, cookies, bread, and buns. Grandmother was happy with the help.

I wanted to help—was there was anything I could do? Would I go and pick berries, (strawberries and raspberries) and apples? Getting some pails from the pantry, I first picked strawberries and then raspberries. Mother came to check on me—it was lunchtime. After lunch, I finished my pail of raspberries and went on to pick apples as well. My next job, in the summer kitchen, was cleaning the strawberries and raspberries, which took most of the afternoon, but I still had to wash and cut up apples if they were to be ready for pies the next day. This was Wednesday.

My uncles wanted to start harvest the next Monday (Sunday was a rest day for all of us). The first harvest was cutting grain as feed for the milk cows. The men would be in the grain for about a month. By early August, they would have it cut and stored for the winter.

It was a busy time in the kitchen keeping up with harvest meals! We made pirogues, baked hams, and cooked beef, pork, and chicken. We also made soup for lunches and, as appetizers, prepared boiled eggs. There were also pickled cucumbers, tomatoes, and peppers to prepare as salad dishes. I also fixed rhubarb for pies and there were cakes for midmorning light lunch.

For breakfast during harvest, my aunt and I would pack everything into the bed of the truck and drive it to the field where it served as a table. We were always sure to include a big container of coffee as well as one of cold water. Arriving in the field, we would blow the horn and park under the trees. After the rest, the men would go back to work. The horses would be resting too, with cold water and grain in grain bags hooked to their harnesses so they could eat and walk at the same time.

At lunchtime, we went back to the field with full meals. Helping was a lot of work—putting out the food (with most times no food left). Then it was back to the house to take the dirty dishes and food containers into the summer kitchen to clean and get ready for the afternoon 'lunch'. The dishes went into the boxes and silverware into containers—knives, forks, and spoons each had a container of their own. We also brought out water for washing hands and faces as well as clean towels each time.

Supper was the last meal we brought out to the field before the men stopped work for the night.

We prepared a special celebration meal at the end of the season. On the first Saturday afternoon, the wives and helpers come over to Grandma's place. Women brought food. Men brought guitars, fiddles, banjos, harmonicas, and accordions. We had a wonderful afternoon and evening—music, singing, and buffet-style food. It was wonderful. I was sad when everyone went home—we would be going home too.

Volunteering to help neighbours

Tina: One of the men asked Dad if I would like to help with the meals on the following week. I looked at Dad and told him Aunt Katie was going to help. Dad said, "Yes."

The farmer was very happy to have me for help. He told Dad that I was a good worker. It was hard work, but something I liked. The job was to start on Wednesday.

On Monday, Aunt Katie and I went over to his farm to see what kind of help was needed from the ladies. We found three ladies at work making pies, doing beans, cakes, and cookies. One woman came into the room to say she couldn't find any berries. I saw the look on the face of the farmer's wife. I asked if I could go to see if I could find any berries. Maybe the woman could get apples and the rhubarb. She said OK.

So we went off, each to her own patch. It didn't take me long to fill my pail with strawberries, and start on another with raspberries. That took a little longer, but when I was done, I went back to the house. The farmer was glad to see me and took the two pails.

His wife said I had done a good job.

I said thank you.

The farmer asked if my aunt had come to help as well.

I told him Aunt Katie was helping in the kitchen. Had the woman finished picking the apples?

No, she had not come back. He had seen her walking back home.

I said I would go get the apples and rhubarb. Also, was there anything needed from the garden—. perhaps I could find a few ripe tomatoes, a few cucumbers, and a couple of onions to dress up the table for supper.

He said that was a good idea. Aunt Katie and I should stay to supper.

We had hot buns, ham, tomatoes, cucumbers, onions, and hot apple pie for dessert. I had picked a pail of apples as well as an armful of rhubarb. The farmer had helpers fixing the harness and checking the wagons—getting them ready for harvest. So those men also stayed for supper.

This was how a farmer got his grain in for the animals. If you helped him, when the time came for bringing in your grain, he would help you. Some men helped with harvesting even though they had no fields of their own. They said the meals were more than enough repayment for the work they were donating.

When the last farmer's fields were finished, there was an interlude of rest.

Harvesting

Richard: The grain harvest was next. The grain was cut with a binder pulled by three horses and put into sheaves that had to be stood up into stooks to dry. This was hard work, and the stooks had to be left to dry, then hauled and stacked for later threshing. The thresher went from farm to farm, and each farmer came and helped each other through threshing time. The threshing machine was usually a (Hallis)? Made in Summerside. The straw had to be forked up into the loft, which was the toughest job of all, and one nobody wanted. When the loft was full, that was usually it, until later. Our job as kids was to dump the baskets of grain that came out the spout from the thresher to the granary. Our next thresher was called a blower which blew the straw up into the loft or into a pile outside. The grain had to be bagged from the thresher. A big step was when three of us bought one of these new machines from Compton Bros. in Morell. I got to take it home, and I was sixteen years old.

Potatoes were next—more hard, hard work. We used a MacKenzie beater-digger which would turn out the potatoes with the beater to the side of the row where they were picked by hand into baskets. The potatoes were then dumped into bags or piled on the carts. One picker's job was to dump the baskets. This job always involved six to ten people. The full carts were dumped into the basement of the house. We always had two carts, one being dumped into the basement while the other was being filled in the field. The basement (cellar) worker had to drag the dumped potatoes away from the hatch to the back of the cellar.

Turnips were next, pulled by hand. Some were stored in the cellar, and a lot were shipped out right from the field. I had four sisters who bagged them. My father and I pulled them and threw them into the cart which was dumped at the corner of the field where the girls would bag them. They weren't too happy to be doing this job. We also made a pit of turnips, covered with clay and straw to be shipped in the spring

FISHING

Packing herring

Ida: A favourite time with my Dad happened when I was about six or seven years old, which would be in the early 1950s. I was oh so eager to please him. He was a fisherman, and the herring run came in the late summer. His loaded boat would be tied to a mooring in the harbour, the herring shovelled into a dory, and then rowed to his private wharf. The herring had to be cleaned and salted the same day because of the hot weather, and there was no ice for us to use. We were fortunate enough to have a natural spring beside our wharf to have very cold water to help keep the herring cool.

My Mom and two men did the gutting and rendering to remove the little silver sac and any leftover blood. Then the herring were ready for salting and that is when my Dad needed even me. The first container to be used was a high wooden barrel. Dad coated the bottom with salt and then began packing the herring neatly together, layer upon layer. My job was to fill the bellies with salt, then pass them quickly to him. This would keep them from rotting. Dad would stand me on a crate with a large dish of salt nearby. Sometimes my little hands wouldn't hold enough salt to completely fill the bellies. My Dad never complained and I could tell he was very proud of me.

My Mom brought supper to the fishhouse to save time.

I can still smell those freshly salted herring and the dank fishhouse, but it was not an unkind smell. I can also hear the swishing of my Dad's wet, salty oil clothes as he leaned in and out of the barrels. They were the smells and sounds of a childhood remembrance, a time when the whole family worked together as a means of earning a living.

Boating jobs

Dora: They all went to sea with Pup. I guess he was more of a fireman on that boat—and he not only took my brothers with him and taught them to do all this stuff, but he took the neighbours' kids too that were growing up and a lot of them made a career of it.

My brothers studied and got their engineers' papers. Eddy became Chief Engineer on the gypsum boats and so did Art. Donnie didn't like it so he went one trip to Boston on one of the ships and he came home by train. But Eddy and Art stayed with it and both got through as Chief Engineer. When Art retired he was Chief Engineer over in Amherst at the electrical place for Nova Scotia, or maybe Pugwash? I was never there, but that was where Art finished.

And he couldn't type. That was the funny part of it. And when Art used to type, I'd say, "What are you typing with?"

He'd say, "Two fingers!"—he'd have to do a report or something.

They'd have to go in and write their papers every so often to go through, eh? And Eddy used to have his own room and his own uniform and everything on those ships. Everything just spotless. We were proud of him because he educated himself, right from the bottom up.

Mary: [laughing] And he spent his money on his baby sister!

Dora: Yeah!

Mary: No wonder you're always so well dressed—you're used to it!

Other Jobs

Cordwood

Ethel: In the 1930's I remember my Dad cutting cords and cords of pulp wood and then peeling it to sell. It was then hauled to Montague.

Women's Lib

Peggy: I always worked with my father out in the woods—the old crosscut saw, sawing wood—and I used to say, "How come girls can't go out and work on the road and doin' things the boys do?"

My father said, "Before you're finished in this world, you'll see that they'll all be working. The girls'll all be working." They didn't then, but we done all the farm work: the cattle, cut the hay, and all that kind of stuff.

Lighthouse keeper

[here is where Arlene's stories began about her life growing up in Kincardine, Ontario]

Arlene: I'd like to talk on the lighthouse. Dad started at the lighthouse after the war, the First World War. He'd met Mom over in England.

Mary: Oh, she was a war bride.

Arlene: Yes. But it was a beautiful place to live. So many people think if you're raised in a lighthouse, you're all by yourself but we weren't. The lighthouse was only a block from everywhere.

Mary: I have a picture of that lighthouse I found on the computer.

Arlene: Well there it is right there. [She points to a picture on the wall that shows the lighthouse trimmed in red, on the shores of Lake Huron and with the town, Kincardine, nestled around it]

Dora: Is that where you lived, Arlene? Right in that lighthouse?

Arlene: That's where we lived. There was a tower and then the living quarters were underneath. There was a big kitchen, a big dining room, a big living room and there were three bedrooms—If you went upstairs there was a little sitting area that you could just sit in and look out—it was just beautiful.

When I was young, every morning—we all had our time, we had to go up in the summertime, go right up to the top and pull the blinds. And then in the evening, I had to go up and pull the blinds up and turn the light on. I remember different times it'd just be getting dark and I'd be 'ohhh, I haven't done my job!' and I'd go hoppin' up to do it!"

Mary: How old were you then?

Arlene: Oh, we weren't very old. We all had our own time. And I used to cut all the lawn, even when I worked. I'd come home and cut all the lawn, it was all lawn at the front.

[The lighthouse was situated on the shore of Lake Huron with the harbour in front of it extending out to the channel, which was then bordered by the breakwater. There were sandy beaches and Arlene would run down from her home in the lighthouse and swim the channel.]

I was brought up so close to the water, I wasn't very old and I came down to the shore and Mom said, "Where did she go?" and she found me down there.

And she said, "You've got to learn how to swim right away."

Now I was just about 3 or 4 years old. So I taught myself how to swim.

I asked my sister, "Teach me how to swim."

She said, "You teach yourself."

Mary: As older sisters do.

Arlene: Yes. Dad had to look after everything. There was always power. We had to have power for the lighthouse. And then at the end of the pier was a range light—he'd have to walk up there to put the range light on. If the fog rolled in, you could smell it. You'd wake right up. Then you'd have to go and put the fog horn on. It was interesting.

When I was small, I remember yachts would come in from the States, and the workers who were on there were black. Then there were two (ships), the *Onward* and the *Donald Mac* fishing. This guy wanted a place to stay and Dad said he'd ask—the place was full all the time—and he said, "I'll just stay two weeks," and he stayed two years!

Cashier

Arlene: Mom fell and broke her leg. That suited me just fine.

I said, "I'm going to quit school and help you."

I wasn't a school person. I liked the activities at the school. She didn't want me (to help her). When I was walking past the drug store, I went in. And I knew [the druggist] worked alone and I asked if he wanted help and he hired me. And I got 25 cents an hour.

Mary: [laughing] You and me, starting salary 25 cents!

Arlene: And I teased my friends because some of them were working at Stedman's or whatever and they got 15 cents an hour. I was there until I got married.

Mary: Did you know Ray [Arlene's first husband] from school?

Arlene: No, no. He's from here [PEI].

Mary: Oh, that's right. Both of your husbands were from the Island originally.

Arlene: Yes, I was going to end up on the Island one way or another. The Island didn't mean anything to me then. You heard about it in school.

Dora: I only had my grade 10.

Mary: And, at that time, that would have been normal. So [Dora] when did you come to PEI.?

Dora: '54. It was 1947 when we were married. Henford taught carpentry at the school [in Windsor] after the war.

[The young couple came to PEI. and started Western Tire in Charlottetown. It was a busy time with Dora working in the store with her husband.]

Dora: We came over here and we started our business in town. And I was the one who wrote the letter to get the franchise from Western Tire.

Mary: How old were you, Dora?

Dora: Well we moved over here in '54. I was 18 when I got married. So, well, I never had time to figure it out. So we opened the store and I didn't know anything about it. We were lucky—I didn't expect an answer. The head fella came down, his name was Bush—I don't know his first name. And anyway, every cent of money we had went into the store. In the meantime, we got our apartment and Henford went down to Holman's Department Store and bought something. He only had a few dollars in his wallet and didn't he leave his wallet in the store!

We were coming home and I said, "Hang on to your wallet 'cause that's all the money we have."

And we came home and I said, "I hope you didn't lose your purse."

And he looked and no wallet. There was a fella who worked at Holman's and he had the wallet for him when he went back in after it. I forget his name now, his wife worked there when I worked at Holman's.

But anyway, what I started to tell you—after we sold the store I had to do something. Henford wasn't feeling well; he was sick. He always had the support on his back and couldn't do this, and he couldn't do that, so I applied to go back to school. I went to upgrading in Charlottetown. And I had a great time too, with all those fellas that were upgrading—out in the hallways, having a cigarette—I wasn't but they were! [giggles]

And there was a woman, my age—I forget her last name but her first name was Alice and anyway, I got my grade 12. We got a diploma and everything. So she got a job at the university—and I thought I'd get a job.

Hanford's laughing at me: "You won't get a job."

I said. "Wait and see if I get a job."

So I went into Holman's Department Store and Doreen was there—forget her last name—she was the Personnel Manager. She hired me for the Ladies Wear. So that was fine, I was quite happy.

I was only there for about a week or two and she called me into the office and she said, "I want to have a chat with you."

So I thought, "What's this about? What did I do now?"

She said, "I want to know if you'd go up to the office."

And I said "Me work in the office? I never did that type of work in my life."

And she said, "I want you for Head Cashier."

I said, "What about Pearl? She's second cashier, why wouldn't you ask her?"

She said, "I already did ask her, and Pearl don't want the responsibility. And I know you can do it. So will you try it?"

And I said, "I suppose, I guess I will."

And I was Head Cashier there for a number of years until I quit. So I was up on the third floor at Holman's and there were no guards or nobody there

Work & jobs: Other jobs

Friday nights but yourself and everyone that got paid—Island Tel and all the carpenters and all the people like that, they came up and paid so much on their account and that's how we cashed their checks, eh? It was just like a bank. And I'd have a stack of checks like that [she demonstrated with two fingers held inches apart].

Mary: So six or eight inches of checks!

Dora: I'd have to balance out and Pearl—we worked just like this together, [crossed her fingers tight] and if I was out a few cents, we'd have to go over those checks and maybe we'd have reversed figures, it might have been 95 cents or 90 cents but we'd want to balance out to the cent. She'd balance out first, and then she had to give me all of her money, and then I had to balance out and make up a sheet. Head office was in Summerside so everything went to Summerside.

So if Pearl had a mistake, well, I'd help her and we'd go over the checks together. I'd read it back for her and we'd be checking them off 'til we found it.

Mary: Did you have an adding machine to do that?

Dora: Yep. Then when I balanced out, if I was out a few cents, she'd help me. It was interesting. Mrs. Myers was the head one of the office. Elaine Myers. We just got along like clockwork anyway. We had a lot of fun working there too.

Arlene: Isn't it funny? How you can look back and see the fun in things.

Dora: I could see people coming in and the fella who worked in charge of one department—we had shoes, we had everything in there.

And that woman came up and she couldn't charge something because I'd have to go check her account and see if she owed money and if she was back three months she'd have to pay on it in order to use it again.

I used to wear my hair all up in 'bubbles' at the time—and I said, 'You have to make a minimum payment', and she couldn't do it.

She went downstairs and they said, "Are you going to take it?"

He said, "No, that one up there with the hair on top of her head, she said, "No." Well of course that went all through the store. And we all just laughed. It was a fun time."

[Shared laughter added to the brightness of the room]

Arlene: You could have put it in the paper. So then they'd come up and say, "I want to talk to that one with her hair on top of her head."

[A pleasant pause followed these words as we sipped our tea, our thoughts backwards in time]

Dora: I always got along with everybody like that. And you make friends, forever.

Mary: How old were your kids when you started at Holman's?

Dora: Well, the boys were still home. Barbara was away, I think, at the time. But not real little, I'm not sure how old they were.

Leaving for work

The Depression Years

Arlene: Well, you know right after the war (WW1), the Depression hit, in the 30's. Things were not good. Before he got the job at the lighthouse [in Ontario], a whole bunch of them would jump a train and go out west to work and then come back.

Dora: I can remember Percy saying there used to be a crowd from the Island go out west.

Arlene: And the kids then, they didn't go to school. Just a few grades and then they had to work.

Dora: And you take the Island here. She was isolated way, way back. And now there's the Bridge.

Mary: And you can come and go as you please!

Arlene: And you talk to different ones and they'd maybe get to Charlottetown once a year. And that would be it.

Dora: They never got from one end of the Island to the other.

I think that's why so many of them are related around here. If you lived here (Belfast), you might marry someone from Point Prim or Wood Islands but you'd be related to someone around here.

Mary: So it's a good thing that the next generation, so many wives were 'Come From Away'!

[We all laughed and agreed]: New blood!

Dora: Because when you talk to someone from around here, you don't know who they're related to. They are all related, somehow. I've got into a lot of trouble. I wouldn't have said it if I had known.

First time to Ontario

Winnie: In 1951 my boyfriend had gone to Ontario to work. We wrote to each other, and he was always asking me to come to Ontario. A year earlier I had finished grade 11. Circumstances were such that I was not going any further education-wise at the Moment. A friend was going to Ontario on the train and said, "Why don't you come with me?"

In order to share her booth, I had to get a first-class ticket, which cost $37 to go from Charlottetown to Toronto. My Dad and uncle drove us to Charlottetown on Sunday night, and we were going to Toronto the next day.

The last thing Dad said to me was, "As long as there's a roof over my head, you'll always have somewhere to come home to."

That was wonderful and yet made me feel bad for leaving. But off we went. The trip took two days—or two nights and a day—or two days and a night—at any rate, through the night the train whistle would blow—street-crossing or meeting another train or whatever—and I remember thinking the wheels turning said, "Clickety, clack, you can't go back, you can't go back," wondering what in the world have I got myself into?

When we arrived in Toronto, my friend's fiancé met us at the train, but my ticket was to Hamilton. I didn't want to stay on the train by myself, so I got off with them and came by car from Toronto to Hamilton. In the meantime, my boyfriend had met the train in Hamilton, and I wasn't on it. When we got to his place, I could hear fiddle music, so I knew we were in the right place. He was coming in the back door as I went in the front door. Anyway, we drove around the next day, and I couldn't get over the skyscrapers. "You mean people actually live in those places!" I was used to living in PEI. I don't think I'd ever seen a place that had *three* stories, let alone 10 or 15. Then I was looking in the paper to find job applications and whatever kind of thing and then there was a list of *for sale* things. You had to buy everything and that was an eye-opener because at home you had potatoes and vegetables in the basement and hens that lay eggs etc. Then I saw *manure* for sale. [laughter] I read it again to make sure I was reading right.

Yes, that's what it said: 'MANURE FOR SALE'. If I had that pile behind our barn, I could make a fortune. The next big eye-opener was their milk and bread were delivered door-to-door, and the milk company and the bread company gave each person a placard that you put in your window—one side said milk the other side said no milk and the same for bread. This enabled the delivery man to pass your house if you didn't need any that day.

Tom: So this was *each day* they would come by?

Winnie: Yes, each day. We were talking about this, and a friend said, "We often had no bread or no milk but we didn't put a sign in the window to tell everybody."

So I got a job in a 5 & 10, they used to call it back then. My department was housewares. One day I waited on this lady, and after the transaction was over, she said to me, "What part of the old country are you from, dear?" and it nearly broke my heart to tell her I came from PEI and I'd never been out of Canada.

We got married and lived in Ontario for over 40 years, and had our children there and everything else, and I adjusted to their way of life, but it was a big surprise when I first got there.

Returning to the Island

Seizing the time

Tom: Can you tell us about getting back to the Island? Obviously you're here on the Island now. What were the circumstances that had you coming back and how did it feel?

Winnie: Absolutely. Well, we had come different years for holidays, and we had family—both of us were from the Island originally and had family here. My husband had the notion that when he retired he would like to come back to PEI to live so he took early retirement...

Tom: What was his name?

Winnie: Francis McCormick. In the meantime I had gone and taken a course to be a health care aide, and I was working now that the children were all grown up and I loved my work, on top of which I got a pay check every two weeks which was not hard to take, so I dragged my feet for a while. He really wanted to come back to the Island to live, and I thought, well, we've stuck it out until the children are grown up and they're on their own. If we want to do it, we should do it while we're still healthy and can manage for ourselves sort of thing. So if it doesn't work, we can always go back to Ontario, so we came in 1997. We bought a house, and we've been here ever since. For ten years we had a wonderful life, and then his health began to fail, and three years ago he passed away. But I'm still here, and PEI is home.

Tom: I had a friend who told me, "Tom, you need to decide what you still wanna accomplish in life before you're drooling over the edge of a wheelchair. That was a scary kind of image that he painted, so I got busy and ended up with early retirement and moving to the Island. I haven't regretted it at all. Making the most of the time you have certainly is a good piece of advice.

Winnie: The fact that we came back to the Island certainly was the best decision we ever made, because my husband played the violin or fiddle, and old-time music had gone out of favour in Ontario. It was still very much a way of life on the Island. He got to play for benefits, Cèilidhs, provide musical back-up on CDs, and he could go fishing if he felt like it, which he'd always remembered doing and didn't have the chance to do in Ontario. If he decided at supper time to go to a dance, well, we could just wash our face and go. I have no regrets about coming. I console myself with the fact we had those years together, and no one can take that away from me. I'm grateful that we did have that and that I still have my health and one day at a time.

Moving to PEI

[Arlene reflected back on the time she and her second husband, Don, moved to PEI. They'd vacationed there with Arlene's youngest son, Doug.]

Arlene: I just loved it here. [It was on their way back home that the decision was made.] We hit the 401 on Labour Day and it was bumper to bumper.

And I said to Don, "Let's move to the Island."

That's all I had to say. He had the place up for sale the next week.

[We laughed with her]

Arlene: When I came here, I didn't know anyone. It also took Don a while to settle in. After we built the house, he mentioned going back. And I told him 'Everyone, no matter what happens—a death or whatever, give yourself two years. In two years, if you want to go back, we'll go back.'

And then he was able to settle in. Some of his friends that he knew from here were already up in Ontario and the ones that he came back to, you have to get to know them again after all those years apart.

I still feel like I'm from away, to a point—I'd meet so many, and I couldn't remember their names—who were friends of Don. But I like the Island. I just love everything about it.

It's very, very similar (to Kincardine).

Dora: You're surrounded by water.

Arlene: Yes, And the weather up there is the same as here. You get nice summers and you can get lousy winters. My Mom found it hard because she came from a big city and when she hit Kincardine, there was no power (then) and the outhouse and then the bad winters.

There was one time that the sun came out, and she said, "It's gonna clear!"

I said, "No, it's just ready to take another wallop!"

Which it did!

Yankees from the States

Winnie: We always called them Yankees. Grandma had two brothers and a sister who married and lived in the United States, and periodically, usually in the summer, they would come home for a vacation, and it was like the king and queen coming, because Dad would kill a couple of chickens, Mom would cook them, and she would make potato salad, and at that time she made her own salad dressing. She had a bunch of kids to look after, and did her own laundry. They all loved music because grandma was of Irish descent. The men would usually be dressed in Sunday clothes, as we thought, and wore two-tone shoes, and they drove a car, and one cousin—Dad's cousin had a little girl and no little ones at that house, so we would be made—it was insisted that we go to play with this little girl. She was a bossy thing—she was younger than we were, but she was bossy—she always had to be whatever it was. We went upstairs for something—for a doll or something—and looked in the bedroom doorways and the ladies were having a nap in the afternoon! Well, this was unheard of. Like the only time my mother ever was in bed in the afternoon was when the children were born. So for years I thought these people must be awfully rich, and then I went to Ontario to live, and realized that people worked all year to get this two-week vacation in the summer. They were just ordinary people the same as the rest of us.

MEDICINE

DOCTORS

Country doctor

Richard: Dr. Pres MacIntyre—he was a—what you call a Doctor back then. He done everything. Did you ever hear people talking about him?

Tom: No, I haven't

Richard: He operated on people, and he delivered babies—which they don't do now. Now all they do is write up a prescription. He used to go out on calls through the country—delivered babies on kitchen tables and the whole bit. So anyway, I used to take my Father to him—2 Bucks—that's what he charged—2 Bucks.

Tom: The Government didn't subsidize that....

Doctor as dentist

Dora: My sister (Lorena) went in training for a nurse. She was four years older than me. And she's the one that's still in the nursing home in Toronto. But when she went in nursing, she had to have her teeth fixed. There was no money to go to the dentist—that was never even thought of, so Dr. Heinz froze her—she sat in a chair in the kitchen and I was scared to death, and he froze her and she had them all out at once. In the kitchen!

She was just sitting on a hard chair. And I was crying and he said to me, "You'd better get out of here or you're the next one!"

I'll never forget it. And I went out and sat on the doorstep.

And that same doctor pulled my tonsils out—at the house.

Arlene: [laughing] Everything was done at the kitchen table back then. I don't really remember, but I know they took the kitchen table upstairs, and took all the curtains and the blinds off the windows. I know I was on the kitchen table, and I don't know what happened after that. He took my tonsils and adenoids out.

Dora: [thinking for a minute] I told that to my (own) doctor once and he said, "I believe you, the old doctors used to do all that." Can you imagine, Mary?

Mary: [laughing] The chance you were taking—bleeding so much you died, or infection....

Dora: It was unbelievable! Just unbelievable.

Mary: At the time, it was just the way things were done.

Arlene: That's right.

Dora: And my brother Art—he wasn't supposed to be driving the bicycle, this old rusty bicycle, that had no fenders on it and he got his leg caught in the chain. So he never told anybody —and he ended up with lockjaw. The same doctor, Dr. Arthur Hines, came to the house and he went upstairs and when he seen what was wrong with him, he wrapped him up in an old car blanket on the bed and took Art right to the hospital. Took him to Halifax, himself.

Mary: How did they get to Halifax—a car or a horse and buggy?

Dora: It was a car; he'd be one of the first to have a car.

Secretly removing a scar

Tina: I have only one memory of my sixteenth birthday. I was at home, the girls were invited—there were six of us. Around our place at the church we had the piping around for them to tie the horses and stuff when they came to church and underneath, because we had calves, we had wire. Three of us were sitting—I was in the middle and two girls—one on each side. The boys were standing around bugging us, so one of the girls decides she's going to jump off. As she jumps off she throws her arms back and I didn't have time to grab ahold of the bar. I go over on the barbed wire, ripped my shoulder all to pieces, went inside and showed it to Mom and said, "Can you do something with this?"

My father looks at me and says, "Well if you'd of done the dishes instead of going out playing birthday, you wouldn't have gotten hurt."

Barbara: Condolences, right?

Tina: I didn't like him very much that day.

Tom: I can imagine.

Tina: Yes, and when I reached—a couple of months later—my Dad had given me a couple of nylon blouses for my birthday, and every time I wore them I noticed the boys were looking at my back all the time, so I figured, 'Why do they keep looking at it?' Then I remembered the scar was back there. It was that wide and that long [gesture not recorded] and I was wondering, 'What am I gonna to do with it?' because I didn't like that. So one day I decided I was going to go see the doctor. I walked a mile, caught the bus 7 miles into town, went to see the doctor. Nobody at home knew about it—none of my parents knew about it. I went to see him.

He says, "What can I do for you?"

I showed him my back and I says, "Can you do anything with this?"

He says "Come back a week from now."

The following week, back again. Walked a mile, drove the bus seven miles, went into the hospital.

He says, "Take your shirt off."

I took my shirt off. He pulled my strap down. I was lying on my stomach. He comes over to the edge of the table.

He says, "Are you sure you want to go through with this?"

I said, Yes, I don't like people staring at me all the time."

So now I've got just a wee tiny line down my back.

Barbara: What'd he do? Sew it up?

Tina: He took it out—he operated. He took the scar out and sewed it together. I hadn't told anybody. I paid him—it cost me $5, which is a little different price from today. So then I went back by bus again to the corner, and then I got off and started walking, but my two baby brothers, they were used to coming up to me and I always grabbed ahold of the older one on my left arm and the younger one on my right arm. My mother had walked up with them because she wouldn't let them go on the road. Walter was fine, he was safe he was the second youngest he came up to my shoulder but when I went to pick Nick up I just dropped. Now there were 10 stitches back there. I was supposed to go back a week later to get the stitches removed. So Mom had taken a step further behind me and she saw the blood running down the back of my shirt.

She said, "*What* did you do to yourself?"

I said, "Well, I got tired of everybody lookin' at me and pointing at my back with the scar when I was wearing nylon shirts."

She said, "*You didn't*"

"Yes," I said, "I had the doctor remove it."

So when we got home she pulled it together—taped it together—and fixed it up. The following week I went back he took all the stitches out.

He said, "Beautiful except for that one there."

Illnesses and diseases

I fight polio

Tina: I had been working in Winnipeg for Dr. K. several months. When my mother came to visit me, I would go home for a visit every second week. I was surprised when she called asking if we could have lunch on Saturday. My answer was, "Yes."

When I saw her, I knew that something was wrong. I waited for mother to tell me. What a surprise—she was expecting a baby. She needed my help. Three days later, I left Winnipeg and Dr. K., with his understanding of my mother's need.

Thursday I came home. Friday I cleaned the house. Saturday I washed clothes. Sunday after church, we went for lunch at the aunt & uncle's place. There were several children present. One of the boys was in a wheelchair I asked him what had happened. He said that he fell. However, he was told he would get better. I had played catch with him since baseball was out of the question

We found out a few days later that he had polio.

Monday I was feeling a little under the weather and there was quite a big snowstorm.

Tuesday, Mother was sick. Dad said he would have to take her to the hospital. There were two big snowbanks in the driveway. I got dressed, picked up a shovel, and went outside to clear the snow bank. I had finished the first one and was about three feet into the second when Dad came out to see how I was getting on. Mother had to go now! I quickly dug a path to the passenger door and went in to help bring her to the car. I sat my baby brothers on a chair and told them to watch the car ride through the snow

I knew Dad would need me to push it they were to get through the second snow bank.

"Don't worry about anything at home," I told him.

After he got through the snow bank and checked back on me, all he could see was a hand wave—I had fallen into the snow.

Back in the house, I found the two boys laughing at me for falling into the snow. I was still not feeling good—weak and dizzy. I knew it was not from pushing the car. The boys played quietly on the floor. When Dad came home, I sensed something was wrong. He had tears in his eyes. "Things aren't good," he said.

Once the boys were in bed I asked what was the matter. He said he had a choice. He had to choose between Mother and the baby. He looked at me and asked what he should do. I was 16 going on 17. My choice was that the boys needed their mother more than they needed another baby. Dad asked me if I would stay home and look after my younger sister and the two boys.

It required no thought: "Yes."

He still had to report the decision to the doctor.

The next morning when Dad called me to get up so he could go to work, I said, "Yes," I was awake. I called Ann, my sister to get up and go down to eat and get ready for school. She was upset that I was staying in bed, but I couldn't feel anything from my waist to my toes and couldn't move. From the waist up, I was OK. Ann went downstairs and reported I was not getting up and said I couldn't move my legs. Dad came up and asked if I was OK.

"I can't move my legs."

Unknown to me, he had a pin and pricked both legs with no response—there was the proof.

"Stay in bed while I take Ann and Walt to school."

The baby, Nick, hearing he would be taken next door, which he disliked intensely, began to cry.

"I'll look after Nick," I told Dad, "If you will help me downstairs."

He said he would think about that. I tried to get dressed—it was a lot of trouble, but in the end I managed. Now, how to get downstairs? From the bed, I could reach the clothes closet. Then, by pulling my legs one at a time

Medicine: Illnesses and diseases

with my hands, I was able to drag myself to the stairs. I dreaded falling. I grabbed the banister and pushed one leg down and then the other. It was a very slow trip!

Next there was the hallway to navigate. It was very difficult to hang on to the wall. When I got to the basement door, it was open and I couldn't reach it to close it. On the other side of the hallway was the wood cook stove that provided heat for the house—very hot. This is where Dad found me.

"What are you doing here?" he asked.

He picked me up and took me to the kitchen. I reiterated I would look after Nick, so he didn't have to go next door, and that stopped his crying.

While I was drinking the coffee Dad brought me, I began to cry from pain in my legs and waist. Life began to come back from the waist down. I didn't mind the pain since it seemed to signal I was going to be OK. After taking Walt and Ann to school, Dad went on to work.

I cleaned up the breakfast dishes and then discovered there was not enough bread for lunch, so I made some bread. I set the dough and when it had risen, I made three dozen buns. Bless God, I had my legs back.

But Dad did not tell mother about my legs—it was left to me to tell her after she came home.

Snowmobile trip for appendicitis

Miriam I remember my sister having appendicitis, and they had to go to the neighbours. Dr. Hobb was in Newtown and at the time—no he wasn't—Dr. Stewart was in Eldon and they had to get him—met him down at the end of the road with the horse and sleigh, and he took the *Skidoo* and took her into town and operated.

[?]: *Skidoos* back then?

Miriam: Well they called it a snowmobile. She was only 14. A year later I went in and had mine out.

Barbara: Did you phone first—did you phone for the doctor?

Miriam: Probably—I was sick for 2 weeks with the pain before they ever took me. It was almost ruptured.

Tom: So what hospital were you taken to?

Miriam: Prince Edward Island Hospital in Charlottetown.

Tom: So it was a long trip?

Miriam: 25 miles

Tom: By *skidoo*?

Miriam: Maybe he crossed—I don't know how he went—whether he crossed the ice or what he did—I don't know.

SELF-SUFFICIENCY

LAUNDRY AND CLOTHES

Clothes barrel treasures

Winnie: They [relatives from the States] used to send barrels of clothes home once a year. They'd go back to the States and they'd send a barrel of clothes—usually women's clothes because those men—Dad was a wiry little man, and those men were heavy-set guys so none of their clothes—maybe a shirt, but grandma was pretty good to sew so she could alter things. The women's dresses, she would rip them up, and sew them back up, and make dresses for us girls when we were little. It was a godsend really, because with these resources then they could—at that time the boys wore something called breeches—they were like riding breeches, and they went down to mid-calf and they had laces on the side and they used to wear long, woollen socks,

In the winter time we wore lumbermen's rubbers. They were dreadful things—your feet are always cold. You didn't take them off when you went to school—you had them on your feet all day. The boys' had bumpy soles on them but the ladies' were smooth and they were even colder. At that time too women or girls always wore dresses. you could wear ski pants, but you had to wear a dress/skirt out over the top of the ski pants. That was the style back then. In the one-room school, the people who sat beside the stove got too warm and the ones on the outer side of the room got too cold, so there never was a happy medium.

Beating rugs

Mary Ellen: Rugs and mats had to be taken outside and placed on the clothesline. The dust had to be beaten out with a broom. The laundry was done on a washboard by hand before we could afford a gas washer. In the winter time our clothes were dried behind the stove on a wire rod.

Scrub board

Dora: Mother, Olive, did the wash with a scrub board. Later on, she had a wringer washing machine. She heated the water in the wood stove in a big copper pot. The boys would haul the water from an open well.

Arm in the wringer

Miriam: I was still washing by hand later when I had three children of my own. In my childhood my mother had a tub that we swung back and forth [to agitate]. We had to do the laundry before we went to school. She'd have the water all hot and we'd be out in the yard and pushing it back and forth.

After that, we had a gas washing machine, inside. You just started it with the gas. Just an ordinary washing machine—you put the wash through the wringer. You had to turn the wringer by hand—wait there was gas, so it must have run the wringer too.

Tom: What about the exhaust from this?

Miriam: We did it out on the porch, but inside.

But one time when I was using one—a wringer washer—my daughter was putting a little cloth through—baby stuff—and her arm went in with her fingers—instead of hitting the release I ran it back, but she was fine. And she just—it swelled a bit. My Mother-in law and Father-in-law lived in the other end of the house so she went crying to them but she was fine. She was only little. The bones were so soft it didn't affect her any, but...

Tom: [chuckle] Does she still tell that story?

Miriam: Yeah. I guess so. She remembers it. I remember one time my Mother got her hair caught in the wringer, but somebody was right there to release it. I don't know how that happened, but that was the story.

Tom: What came after this?

Miriam: As soon as we got electricity, we had electric about 1958 or '59

Tom: Did you immediately switch to an electric washer?

Miriam: NO! It was years before I had an electric washer. We couldn't afford one. Never had an electric dryer, even when I had 5 children. Not 'til after

Self-sufficiency: Laundry and clothes

they were grown up. There were no electric dryers at first.

Wringer washer

Ethel: I remember my Mother washing in a washtub, getting her water out of the pump and heating it on the stove every Monday. Every Monday. Monday was her wash day.

Tom: Now when you said 'washtub' this wasn't a wringer type?

Ethel: No, by hand!

Tom: By hand!? So what were the steps—you dump it in the water—and then what?

Ethel: You had to scrub it on a scrub-board

Tom: And where was the scrub-board?

Ethel: In the tub! (stupid)

Tom: On the edge of the tub? I've never—ever....

Ethel: The water's in there, the clothes are in there....

Tom: And after you got finished scrubbing them—what did you do then?

Ethel: You'd dump that water out—put clean water in and rinse them.

Tom: And rinse them. And then what?

Ethel: Hang them on the clothes line.

Tom: Now did you have to wring the water out somehow?

Ethel: Oh yes by hand. Don't you remember those days?

Tom: No—No.

Ethel: You're not that old?!

Tom: Well, hand washing may have been going on here, but, to the best of my memory, where I grew up in Connecticut in the late '40s there were washing machines.

Ethel: We didn't have one at that time. Probably not before I was 10?

Tom: Probably? OK, So how long?

Ethel: Don't remember how long. It took her—but quite awhile. We had four beds.

Tom: So you washed the sheets every week?

Ethel: Yes. Every week we did them.

Tom: Were there families that were not as clean as yours?

Ethel: Oh, no. Everybody did the same thing. There was no other way.

Tom: Except for bachelors who lived in filth....

Ethel: There were no bachelors in my community, growing up.

Tom: You said you got a 'wringer washer' when you were about 10?

Ethel: No just a regular washer. You turned the handle and wrung the clothes out. Then you hung them out on the line—winter or summer—freeze your hands.

Tom: You remember that?

Ethel: Yep—We froze 'em.

Tom: Did the clothes dry when they froze?

Ethel: Well they would freeze, and you would take them in the house and put them behind the stove. And then they'd dry. Most of the water would be out of them—there'd be sun. The sun used to shine then, you know, kind of warm the sheets in the daytime, unless it was raining or a damp day. That was the only way they could dry them.

Tom: That was the next step up from just squeezing them by hand.

Ethel: That's right.

Tom: I've seen the kind [of washing machine] where there was an agitator in the tub and a motor-wringer up on the side.

Ethel: That was a little later in life.

Tom: You said something happened when you were about 10—something came along?

Ethel: Yes, the hand wringer.

Tom: But the wringer was separate from the tub?

Ethel: Yes. You know you turned the handle like this?

Tom: So—nobody lost fingers in that?

Ethel: They could have.

Tom: Not like in the motorized ones?

Ethel: No.

Monday is wash day

Tom: So did you also do all your washing on Mondays?

Miriam: Yes, then it was always Monday. Today it's any day.

Tom: How much of the day do you guess it took? When you were little, you went off to school?

Miriam: Well Yeah. We did the wash and our Mother looked after it. After we were done working at it, she hung it up on the line.

Tom: Did she wring it out?

Miriam: No there was a wringer on the tub that you turned by hand. She'd have to pump water from the Barn and put the water on the stove in a great drum and heat the water.

Tom: On a wood stove?

Miriam: And then pour it into the tub, and then we'd do our wash.

Tom: How much water do you guess she carried—was it a couple of buckets?

Miriam: Oh yeah. We carried buckets for years—from the pumphouse to the house for all uses for water, for drinking—for everything.

Tom: How far away do you think it was?

Miriam: Be from here to the Barn over there [pointing out the window].

Tom: So—a couple of hundred feet?

Miriam: Yeah, yeah.

Tom: And you didn't think anything of it—

Wash/electrification

Arlene: So just keeping the wash done, and doing the dishes and cooking meals was all [my mother] could handle.

Dora: And they didn't have all the conveniences either.

Arlene: That's right. I can remember the old wringer washer machine.

Dora: Lots of people used to get their arms caught in the wringer. Lucky we didn't.

[Arlene remembered doing a wash before power came to PEI.]

Arlene: When we came here first, Ray was just a year old. We came here for Christmas. There was no snow at all, it was warm. It was beautiful. I was outside and it was the [washing] machine with a handle on it—one at one end and one at the other—and you swished it [by hand]. They had no power at that time. It was in the 50s. They were just starting to get power in some places when we moved here."

Dora: We had this old house wired after we came here.

Winter survival

Food in the cellars

Tina: When the cold weather came, it was time to get ready for winter. The job mostly fell to the women. Back then, people used various methods to preserve food over the winter. They canned vegetables, beans, carrots, corn, and so on. They pickled cucumbers, peppers, beets, chow and so on. They dug out the potatoes, dried them, and stored them in the cellar. They braided onions and garlic and they were hung up... in the cellar. They cut cabbage into fine slices and made it into sauerkraut... a fermenting process that took a month or two, depending on the age of the cabbage.

A trip to the cellar in winter was like a trip to the grocery store! There were the shelves of jars: pickles, vegetables, and canned meats, including chicken. There was the sauerkraut, now cured and in jars. There were the potatoes in two big bins... white ones in the bigger and red ones in the smaller. There were the fresh carrots stored in bushel baskets with some garden dirt to keep them crisp.

Then it was back to school until next spring when the process would start all over again... the life of a farmer.

Stocked up for winter

Miriam: There was always plenty of food in the house. There was always canned meat, etc. That was all looked after. We all had out own vegetables.

Tom: What sort of vegetables would be kept over the winter?

Miriam: We'd have cabbage—There would be chicken-wire hanging from the ceiling—the cabbage would be on it.

Tom: In the basement?

Miriam: Yes. It was a clay basement. We had turnips and carrots, but we never had any broccoli back then or cauliflower—I never heard tell of it anyway.

Tom: Certainly—they wouldn't keep through the winter.

Miriam: Yeah.

Tom: So when would you get a Freezer?

Miriam: Not yet! Freezers came later.

Gardening

Big gardens to weed

Dora: Dad had a big, big garden. And Mom would get things out of it, but she never helped. She was in the kitchen.

Mary: Yes, that's right. We were always supposed to weed one row of the garden. But the rows were about 18 feet long—it was a long, narrow back yard. You'd get a third of it done and just give up.

Mom's baking

Mary Ellen: Saturday was homemade molasses and beans. Mom spent a lot of time baking bread, molasses cookies, sugar cookies, cakes, white and dark fruit cakes, biscuits, bannocks, and apple and mincemeat pies. In the summer we would go pick wild strawberries and blueberries so Mom could make us a cake.

What did your mother say?

Dora: Mother had a beautiful flower garden and we all had to do our work. Push the old lawn mower and do all kinds of stuff before we could go anywhere or play.

But I remember when my mother said, "No," we'd go to ask our father. [laughter] And he'd say, "What did your mother say?" and that's as far as it'd go.

We had no money but we had lots of love. We all cared for each other and just the other day, my sister, Lorena, in a nursing home called me and said 'Dora, I don't think we ever had bad words together.'

So I believe we were always taught to care and respect each other.

Dora: What does that sound like?"

Arlene: That's good.

CARE FOR THE ELDERLY

Taking in relatives

Mary: [being an inquisitive journalist, I had to ask for more details] Your niece, Joan came to live with you—how did that come about?

Dora: My brother John was married and his wife Hilda was the first Apple Blossom Princess from Windsor. I don't even remember her; she died at the hospital after Joan was born. So Joan came home and lived with us, and she was brought up as a sister. I was six years old when Joan came to our place.

Arlene: Yes, she's more like your sister that your niece.

Dora: I had a sister Hazel. I can remember Joan's mother playing the piano, but I don't remember my sister Hazel. So she was married and she had two children, Olive and Ethel were their names. Ethel is my age and Olive is two years younger. My sister died, she had a goitre.

My mother and my other sisters told me that Hazel had to go to Halifax to have an operation. And so she died during that operation. So those two girls were brought home and stayed with us until their father re-married, three years later. They whined and cried, they didn't want to go with their father.

They did go live with their father and his new wife, but the kids were never happy, and she would never allow them to come home with us because she was jealous of the family. We couldn't keep in contact with the kids at all, really. But now, once their father died things were different. Now they are all friends with his other children and with us, too. So it all turned out O.K.

Self-sufficiency: Care for the elderly

My mother had Joan and those other two besides—that's eighteen kids.

Mary: Eighteen kids. [I couldn't even imagine the care that took.]

Dora: My father used to get up early in the mornings—I could just keep going!

When we lived in Summerville, I was a kid then, he'd go pick berries. And he'd have a pot of raspberries or blackberries—we had a lot of blackberries, I remember and we'd have a bubble of berries for breakfast.

[The three of us discussed these memories that would come back all of a sudden, just click in and feel like they happened yesterday. Dora looked off in the distance, her eyes not seeing us and her mind alive with times forever gone.]

Nana as family

Tom: Another subject area no one has talked about: did you have older family living with you at home that you took care of as a family?

Corena: I did, my grandmother lived with us from when I was born; I think Nana was there—my mother's mother. I was nine when she passed away. I was very close to her. Her bedroom was downstairs, because she didn't go up stairs. They made a bedroom out of one of the rooms that was on the first floor, and Nana—I remember this—she had a big trunk. In there she had different things—I'd say cards or things that people had sent her. We weren't to touch. When Nana took us in the room, that was fine, but we weren't supposed to otherwise. I'd have to be after my brother for that too 'cuz he didn't listen. She was very special to me. I could remember getting so cross at him because in our kitchen—it was a good sized kitchen—and there was a rocking chair and that was Nana's, and he'd get in that. Nana was somewhere else, and I'd try to push him out so that Nana could get in her chair.

Tom: Was she sort of a babysitter at times?

Corena: Well, yes. On a small farm there there's sure lots to do. They made their own butter—so many things. As I say it was a small farming operation. My Dad was a butcher, and he had a shed across the road where he used to butcher and then go through the country delivering—go around selling meat. But it was special to have her there. I've always been thankful that she was because I had a great relationship with her and was terribly upset when she passed away.

Tom: That's interesting because I've been told this was more the case—nowadays you're sent off to a nursing home or something like that, and there you are.

Corena: No, even when she took quite sick—I think possibly a stroke that she took—and Mom had to try to get some help—people around that were like practical nurses or whatever—people that did that sort of thing—come and stay at night because Mom couldn't do it all day and all evening.

Let me die in peace

Winnie: My mother passed away in 1948. My younger sister was born in '47 and Mom never came back out of the hospital. My baby sister went to live with my maternal grandparents and Daddy's mother was looking after us. She was 70-some-odd at the time. Anyway a year-and-a-half later she got tired or sick or whatever and took to her bed, and nobody really knew what was the matter with her. She would say to me when they'd be taking her up and changing her bed or whatever, "I'm an old woman now, Winifred. Can't you make them leave me alone and let me die in peace?"

She passed away at home in July of 1949. She was 76, I believe. Now that I'm past that age, I can't imagine one of my children landing on my doorstep telling me their wife had died and I was gonna have to look after six or seven children with no modern conveniences or anything else. It nearly drives me crazy thinking about it!

LANDMARKS

BUILDINGS

Museum, caskets, and dry goods

Tom: Here's another topic that we have: landmarks that you see—that you still remember from long ago. What come to mind? Buildings?

Ron: There's an old stone house over in Clyde river that I remember as a kid, still there, made of native Island stone.

Tom: Island Stone? Okay the red soft stuff.

Pat: There's one of those at Lower Montague too. Been there forever.

Ron: There's one I can remember too.

Tom: And you can remember long, that's the point. How about the thing that's the museum in Montague now, that building—what did that used to be?

Pat: That was the post office, many years ago.

Tom: Even before that it was something else, I remember hearing.

[?]: It was the customs house, something I vaguely remember, because it was on the river and boats would come in and that would be the customs house, but don't quote me on that.

Richard: I'm ashamed to say I was never in that museum.

Ron: Neither was I.

Richard: I'm interested in that stuff but I never got into it yet, and I better get goin' too!

Pat: I worked there.

Tina: I went in there once, and the smell in there—I went through the whole thing 'cause my brother was visiting and he and his wife wanted to go and see it. So I went in with them. I was in there five minutes, and I was out. I looked to see where my brother was—I'm glad he wasn't right beside me because he would have turned around and followed me out. At least they got around the whole thing—upstairs, downstairs, and the main floor. I just saw a little on the main floor, and went out the door 'cause the smell of the leather affected me right away. I waited 'till they came out. I wasn't pushing them. I had a place to sit down and Stewart and Beck's was right there. I kept an eye out for them to come out.

Tom: Wasn't there a grocery store up the road on the same side?

Pat: Clark's.

Tom: Wasn't it groceries?

Pat: It was groceries as well as dry goods—they sold everything there.

Richard: Clark Brothers over in Mount Stewart too

Tom: Were they there a very long time?

Richard: Yup.

Tom: Like from your youth?

Richard: Oh yeah.

Pat: Can I talk about the museum? I worked a couple of summers at the Montague Museum and it was fascinating. My job was to catalogue. I would be given some sort of object and I would have to enter it in the book, and then get this fine little white pen and mark the number on it to correspond with what I'd entered in the book. And one summer we put on a display to do with all the businesses that had been in Montague. Sort of antiquities. So

we got the museum all dressed up and a couple of us in long skirts and period costumes to show people around, and the theme was The Old Businesses. So we had several old people that had memories. One woman sat all afternoon and used the spinning wheel so that the visitors could see how that worked. We had a blacksmith with an old, patient horse, and the horse got shod and re-shod all day, and he was just patient. I was showing a group of children around from a school, and they were quite fascinated with this horse—they just spent hours watching the blacksmith and then they came inside, and we had a display of McKinnon Brothers. They made caskets and their store was next to Clark's, if I remember.

Richard: No, on this side of the bridge right across from the post office.

Pat: Right, okay. So they make caskets forever; I mean they were even burying people when I was here a number of years ago, until they finally went out of business.

Tom: Nobody to bury anymore?

Pat: Their methods were a little antiquated shall we say. Anyway to get back to this, they had put in a darling little casket about three feet long, obviously meant for a child and we had that all set up, and I was showing these children around, and they followed me around and their faces were awestruck when they saw this little casket. I gave them my spiel about how the McKinnon brothers made caskets. A lot of their caskets were taken to Halifax after the Halifax Explosion. They sent a lot of caskets there to bury people. Well the children listened to this story, but they had their eyes on this little casket.

I said, "Now, I suppose you want to know about this casket."

They said, "Yes."

So I said, "Well it was for a little child."

So they all said "Yes." They all kind of cuddled a bit closer to each other.

And I said, "Now, would you like to see inside this casket?"

Oh, there was a big gasp and they all gathered close, so I carefully raised the lid and of course there was nothing inside, but, oh, I had my Moment there. Then we went on to the display of Dr. McIntyre's surgical tools. One of the things that he used to do was go around to the schools in the spring and scoop everybody's tonsils out. Believe it or not, there was a black and white picture of the children on one of the schools on the slope and they were laying there and the caption read that they had all had their tonsils scooped out by Dr. McIntyre, and there was the actual tonsil scoop—pretty gruesome, but it was a really fun afternoon.

Tom: But you didn't take out any tonsils?

Pat: No, I wasn't required to take out teeth or tonsils.

Richard: Where did he get time to do all that stuff he done? Now there's 8 or 9 of them over there, or 10 and all they do is write a prescription.

Pat: You got that right.

Richard: He delivered babies on kitchen tables.

Pat: Oh, gosh, yes. He did operations.

Richard: He traveled by horse and sleigh through snow storms and everything. And he charged two dollars.

Pat: If they couldn't pay…

Richard: He never got paid.

Pat: And he had to get paid in lobsters and potatoes.

Richard: It's his truck I have.

Tom: Oh you spoke about him before.

Pat: He was a very interesting person.

Ron: Dr. Ellis was the one we had up our way similar to that. He come to your house and take veggies for pay or whatever.

Credit union and egg grading

Richard: Speaking of credit unions, we had our own Credit Union.

Pat: Where?

Richard: In Vernon River—Cecil Walsh and Agnes—still living—they had it up at their house, and we're used to go there and borrow money, and put money in, and so on and so forth. Another thing—egg grade stations—that's another part of History. H. S. McLeod's had an egg grading and our co-op had egg grading. Every rural—it would be similar in every rural district. Back then that was nothing new. If I wrote about that, it would be just our individual area…

Barbara: That's fine. The thing is that someone would read that and say, "Yeah, we had something like that." It would bring back a whole bunch of memories. They'd love it.

Richard: ...and Callaghan wasn't the first...

Barbara: ...garage...

Richard: ...the building used to be a dance hall in Albury Plains...

Barbara: Yes, I remember that.

Richard: ...and they'd fight and so on and so forth, and when the dances ended there was a man called Sil Purry[?]. He was from up in Evangeline area, married to a local lady, and he started a body shop. Jimmy O'Halloran was 15 years old and he used to drive out on a bicycle and look where he went from there!

Barbara: Jimmy?

Richard: He'd go out on a bicycle to work at the body shop, from Greenfield.

Barbara: Listen, you sharpen up that pencil. You could write a history on Jimmy O'Holleran.

AGING

HOW TIME PASSES

It creeps up

Barbara: [I got a patio set and went to] move it so I could put my umbrella up, so I could sit in the shade and eat my lunch. I went like this [gesture not recorded] and it never moved! What did I crack back there? I can't flip the darn thing. Now when did that happen?

Pat: I don't know. It just creeps up on you.

Barbara: Surprise. I'm not happy about that.

Tom: So old age comes when you're not expecting it?

Barbara: I tell you.

Tina: Mine didn't come when I wasn't expecting it; mine was due to a car accident—a front-end collision, but I couldn't leave the driver get killed. I pulled him off of the steering wheel. And that's where all my [disability came from].

Barbara: I don't think of myself as old. I still think like yesterday, I was in my twenties. When I'm lying in bed in the morning, I feel like I'm in my twenties, and then I go to get up, and I age 50 years!

Pat: Don't make any sudden moves. That's my new slogan.

Barbara: I went into a credit union in O'Leary one day, I had an account up there and I went in and one of the girls in front of her booth had a little poster, and it was this stork with a fish in its mouth, and someone had it by the neck, and it was trying to swallow it and poster said, *Never Give Up.*

Tom: Yes, it's the Frog that is hanging onto the neck so it can't be swallowed.

Barbara: That's right, yeah.

Things look too big

Tom: What I'm hoping for is a section that would just talk about the challenges [of getting old] that you've encountered that you didn't prepare for. I seem to have some arthritis, and yet I find that if I keep going, and keep projects, it helps. I remember a sermon—one of the few sermons I actually remember—we were visiting a church in Niagara Falls, actually, and the pastor was talking—it was Father's day—about how you're only old when things start seeming too big to tackle. I've always hung on to that. His example was Caleb, who at a hundred said, "Hey, all right, we've taken the Promised Land, now we're gonna go and take this piece of it up here."

Joshua says, "Go for it."

You know I guess I feel like when I reach the point where everything looks too big to tackle, *then* I'll be old.

Richard: I've already reached that long ago, my boy.

Tom: You've have reached that? Everything looks too big?

Richard: No, but I've got no interest in doing things I done when I was 50. Whatsoever—haven't got the energy—haven't got the interest.

Pat: You know, the energy is what you lack. I think, "Well, I'm going to do this," and I sit down and think, "I don't really want to do that." That's where my baking—I just quit, because I'd go buy stuff—eggs and stuff—bring it home and think, "I'm gonna make biscuits or whatever," and after I thought about it for a while I'd think, "Oh the [heck] with that, I'll go to McDonald's Bakery and buy biscuits. I just can't be bothered."

Richard: Another thought that crosses your mind is I've been there and done that. That's one of the things that comes to your mind. You look back and say, "Well I've *done* that. Why bother?"

Tom: Oh my, you are old!

Barbara: But then you'd want something else.

Richard: I still have interests, but your interest changes as your age. [Elsewhere under *music* Richard talks about taking up fiddle playing.]

Tom: I'm sure I won't argue with that.

New door opening

Barbara: You know, one day I was living in Alberton and my husband was down here work working—we were doing some renovations on the house. It was one of those days when you're dreary, and down, and out of sorts, and bored, and you know you have a whole bunch of stuff to do that you don't want to do. So the dog was pretty sad 'cause my husband was gone, so I said, "Let's go to Summerside."

He had his own seat in the back of my truck, so he thought that was a great idea and off we went. When we got close to Summerside, what in the name of goodness am I going to do in Summerside? I said, "I think I need new glasses." I went to the optometrist there, and I met the most wonderful man. We had a great talk. I tried on some glasses, and he said to me something very important, because when I was ready to go I thanked him and I said, "You know, you've kind of made my day turn around."

He said, "Look at every person you meet as a new door opening."

I thought, what wonderful advice that was. Every so often something comes along again, and the same thing happens: "Boy, that was another door opening." I just think when we get to a point where everything is old hat, that's when all the new opportunities start. That's when we begin to have new opportunities. I know this [book typing] is a whole new opportunity for me—pain in the rear when I'm sitting there typing it, mind you, but I love being involved in it, and all kinds of things.

Tom: I'm sure I love that you are involved.

Pat: You're never too old to start something. I left home two years ago—just up and took my purse and left. You know I was 83.

Barbara: That's courageous.

Pat: Yeah, I just made up my mind I was going to go, so I left.

Aging

Miriam: When I retired in 1995 I looked after elderly people some and served as president of the 50+ club. I also hooked rugs made quilts to raise money for the club. Now that I'm getting up in years, I seem to have aches and pains. I have great friends and family and my neighbours are excellent. Time is going so fast.

Dancing with Jake

Louise: Being with my grandson Jake is like being in love—the kind of intimacy I've only ever experienced a few times in my life. Every moment is lit up. He is four and I am sixty five, but we seem at the moment to suit each other to a T. I know it will change, is already changing, but I am sometimes stunned by what we share now. I wanted to describe the day I spent with him just before Thanksgiving of this past year. I had flown to Montreal to baby-sit him so that my son and daughter in law could have the weekend off.

Jake and I started out the day by making a list. We sat in our PJs under the covers on a futon couch which was at one end of Liam's study. We had a notebook across our laps, and a proper official pen. The two big things on the list were 1) make a cake for the other grandparents, Sarah and Rob, driving up from Vermont and due to arrive that night to take over the baby sitting, and 2) go to a 4:00 Mass at Notre Dame de Bon Secours (a two hundred and fifty year old church in old Montreal). The list also included "Get dressed" and "Have breakfast." And also "Play with trucks." As we finished our list we had the satisfying sense we would get all sorts of things accomplished while doing exactly what we pleased.

After some vigorous truck playing (the trucks were in trouble, the trucks were saved), we finally pulled on our clothes and walked down to the health food store to get ingredients for the Sarah/Rob cake. I also wanted to see if I could find a remedy to help with the ear pain I feared would beset me on the flight back to Charlottetown. My ears had hurt a lot on the descent coming into to Montreal, painful enough that I hoped for some sort of natural analgesic.

So there we were at the health food store: me talking to the proprietor about ear problems while Jake went off with a miniature shopping cart to get eggs and frozen raspberries for the cake. Only four years old! To find those things he almost certainly had to speak French to someone in the store who could direct him. But he pushed that cart through the aisles like a little pro and found what we needed.

We made the cake in the early afternoon after lots of playing and lunch and a failed attempt at a nap. Jake was kept occupied by some giant stickers we had found in a shop beside the health food store and which he now arranged on his bedroom wall. His preoccupation meant I was able to get the apples chopped with a sharp knife before he entered the kitchen. Our hearts were in the right place, but I can't say that soggy apple/raspberry cake was very good. Still we did it and checked it proudly off our list.

The best part of the day (every part of the day was the best part) was the trip to Notre Dame de Bon Secours. He and I were exuberant. The metro! The big stairs! The roar as the subway came hurtling in! The speed, as we flew through the dark tunnels! At the Champ du Mars metro stop where we got off, the walls of the station were multi-coloured stripes and the whole cavernous space was filled with music, a Brahms cello concerto I think, piped in at full volume. Arms spread wide like a dervish, eyes half closed in mischief and pleasure, Jake danced to the Brahms.

I had brought diversions to help Jake get through the church service: cards, kinder surprise, apple juice, sticker book, pears, cashews, two of his favorite cars, magic markers, note book... He went through every single thing in my back pack, and then settled into scribbling away in the notebook and munching on a pear as the liturgy rolled on. I basked in the beauty of the old church, eighteenth century pinks and golds, above us on the roof, a huge statue of the virgin reaching toward the sea, wearing her halo of stars.

At Holy Communion Jake followed me down the aisle and was spell-bound when the priest gently laid his hands on Jake's head. Inexperienced with church, he became very still and received the blessing with a kind of wonder. Afterwards he wanted to walk up to the priest and get a better look. 'Who is that man in the long black dress who laid his hands on my head?' The priest looked down with kindly amusement at this four year old gazing up at him so intently.

"Was I good?" he asked when we left the church.

"You were super good!" I said swinging his hand in mine.

Back at Champ du Mars metro, a group of buskers were playing the Beatles' *Come Together* at the bottom of the escalator. Jake and I hunched our bodies and began to dance on the escalator as we rode toward the band. They looked up at us—grandmother and grandson. We put our hands on our hips and swayed, bobbed our heads, and shuffled our feet as we glided toward them. They grinned at the sight and played louder, just for us. On the ground level, we danced past them, throwing change into their guitar case as we went by. Then we broke apart and ran toward the subway, just for the sheer fun of it. Why not just run!

But it was awkward when his other grandparents, Sarah and Rob arrived. I feared my intimacy with Jake might be a threat to them, though it was probably the other way around. It was not a competition; of course not! Just that they were taking over. They would get to sit with Jake at the kitchen table and hear what he thought about any old thing. In their presence, what had been entirely natural between Jake and me became a kind of acting; I dared not lose myself the way I did when we were alone. Sarah was conscious of Jake's and my closeness, and I did not want to lay claim on him and shut her out. She is after all a wonderful woman whom I've known since my son Liam was as little as Jake is now. She is a friend of mine, not a rival.

It's just that it's always different when a one-on-one situation shifts to a group. Lots of ways a group is better. But a four year old doesn't necessarily know that. The next morning Jake got into bed with me and we played 'baby and mommy hedgehog'. We were supposedly hibernating— not! There was no way Jake was interested in hibernating, though I clung to my pillow with my eyes shut tight. He squirmed and wriggled and thrashed under the covers as I tried for just a few more minutes of sleep. Sarah came in and sat on edge of the futon with us, but Jake scooted away from her, frowned, and said, "No!" She took this reaction in stride, but I was not happy. After she left, I had to tell him that he couldn't play that way, that it might hurt Sarah's feelings. "You're only four, but I know you understand what I'm talking about." I said.

"No, I don't," he smiled. I was accusing him of wielding power. That thought had to be a little intoxicating.

He and I talked a lot about death that day in Montreal. He was worried that I would die, and he wonders when he will die. He was curious about time too. Knowing that I was sixty five he asked, "How old will you be Nana, when *I* am sixty five?" Later he said suddenly, "I don't want to grow up and be a man and have kids!" Like Peter Pan, he'd rather fly off to never never land where no one gets old or dies, not even Nana... Yet like it or not, his life unfurls before him.

Last summer Jake and his family visited us on PEI. It was late July; he was not yet four. One day when we were picnicking up at Morel, he wandered far down the beach before anyone noticed his absence. Liam went bounding after him and found him in the dunes pondering the spiky dune grass. "What are you doing Jake?" asked Liam. "That grass is prickly; it will hurt your bare feet." When there was no answer, Liam asked, "Are you looking for something?"

With his father's dazed and dazzling eyes Jake gazed out across the sandy hills and said simply, "I'm looking for my life."

A week later, he and his family returned to Montreal; a month after that, he turned four; and then, just before Thanksgiving he and I spent a magical day together in Montreal checking off our list. When I left him the next afternoon, he was distracted from a sorrowful farewell by a kinder surprise hidden in one of his toy trucks. As I walked toward that same metro station we had been to the day before, I felt a lover's heartache. I was on my way up to Toronto to join my younger son Martin for Thanksgiving proper; there was much to look forward to, yet I was weighed down. I missed Jake already, and I couldn't bear to think he might miss me too. I would protect him from every sorrow if I could, including the loss of me.

And now Jake, I realize that in describing that day we spent together in Montreal, I am in fact writing you a letter, one you might or might not read a long time from now. And I just want to tell you this: you are right to see that your life, right *now* is visionary, shining. Carry a fragment of this childhood sweetness into the life you were looking for that day in Morel. Don't forget your list; it's important to get stuff done. But also don't forget to dance. I'll be with you, I promise.

Cultivating friendship

Helen: To grow a friendship you must encourage, support, love, and appreciate that one. Don't overlook the good in that person. If a friend is in distress, offer your unconditional support, your undivided attention, and your shoulder to lean on. When a friend is under criticism or attack, stand up for them—if that friend is in the right. A friend is one who walks in to help when others are walking out.

Friendship is deepened and developed by humour. Laughter is the best medicine. In our daily living, the simple act of extending friendship diminishes grief and increases joy. This is the goal of my own life—to show

Aging: How time passes

laughter and be happy, helpful, and supportive. I want to love a positive attitude—an attitude of prayer and faith in the Lord.

50+ CLUB

Purpose

The purpose of the club is to promote heightened quality of life for seniors through education, recreation, and wellness activities in an environment fostering fun, social interaction, and community involvement.

We welcome new members to join us every Wednesday: line dancing, crafts, cards, mosaics, etc. beginning at 9 AM at the Montague Royal Canadian Legion on Douses Road. Monthly meetings are 11 AM the first Wednesday of each month (except for the Summer months).

Origins

In 1990 a group of seniors got together to organize a senior's club for the Montague area. After many meetings and discussions the '50 Plus Club' started with its first meeting on August 22nd. The first president was Faye Fraser, vice president Ruth Nicholson, treasurer Esther Compton, and secretary was Alice MacPhee. The early activities used space donated by the Montague Legion and

began with a $16,180 grant from Department of Health and Welfare under the New Horizons program. They sponsored many different activities including yard sales, a local 16-seat bus to transport members to the mall and churches, and raffles for quilts. By 2000 they were meeting in St. George's Anglican Church and by 2010 they were meeting in the basement of the Montague

Baptist church. In 2011 they moved to the Montague Legion (in their new location) to take advantage of its wheelchair access.

The club has been growing steadily since its inception. Members have made numerous quilts and hooked mats. Line dancing has been a mainstay. Craft projects have included wreaths and stained glass art. There have been many pot lucks made as well as many card games played and trips taken over the past years, and it starts with good fellowship together.

50+ club: Origins

214 Fifty Plus Memories

Recently the club pursued this book project as a way of preserving memories that are gradually being lost.

www.ingramcontent.com/pod-product-compliance
Lightning Source LLC
Chambersburg PA
CBHW030518080526
44586CB00011B/239